I SHOULD
HAVE BEEN A
HORNBY TRAIN

Other books by Pat Arrowsmith

fiction

Jericho
Somewhere Like This
The Prisoner

verse

Breakout
On the Brink
Thin Ice
Nine Lives

nonfiction

To Asia in Peace
The Colour of Six Schools

I SHOULD
HAVE BEEN A
HORNBY TRAIN

Pat Arrowsmith

Cover art: 'The Carol Singers' by Pat Arrowsmith (watercolour; 1944)
Cover photo by Tony Gay

First published 1995 by Heretic Books (GMP Publishers Ltd.),
PO Box 247, London N6 4BW.
World copyright © 1995 Pat Arrowsmith

A CIP catalogue record for this book
is available from the British Library

ISBN 0 85449 190 2

Distributed in Europe by Central Books
99 Wallis Road, London E9 5LN
Distributed in North America by Inbook
PO Box 120470, East Haven, CT 06512, USA
Distributed in Australia by Bulldog Books
PO Box 155, Broadway, NSW 2007, Australia

Printed and bound in the EU by Nørhaven A/S, Viborg, Denmark

Myself, 2 January 1944 (pencil)

**This book is dedicated to
my long gone brother Peter**

Preface

As a former history student and social worker who for twenty-four years worked for Amnesty International, I have learned the vital importance of source material and direct testimony about past events. Consequently, this story of my childhood up to the end of my schooldays is less a wise-after-the-event collection of current recollections than a compilation of items from my childhood writings that illustrate and reveal what my childhood and I myself at the time were like.

I wrote the basic account relatively recently. It is brought to life by the inclusion of extracts from the very detailed diary I kept between the ages of thirteen and fifteen; excerpts from *Those Happiest Days*, the semi-autobiographical novel about schooldays which I wrote at school when I was fifteen to sixteen; chapters from *Multicolour*, the also somewhat auto-biographical novel — or rather, series of sketches of members of a vicarage household — I wrote when I was eighteen, just after leaving school; and copies of several of my teenage poems and of pictures mentioned in the diary. Neither of the novels was printed at the time, although they both came quite near to being, especially *Multicolour*, which came within a hairbreadth of being accepted by a publisher.

* * *

In all the extracts from my diaries and juvenile writings, I have kept the faulty grammar and misspellings as I wrote at the time.

1

I am a Sunday child...born in a Leamington Spa vicarage just in time for lunch on March 2nd 1930. Whether or not I was breast-fed I am not sure, nor whether in any case this would have been significant. My parents wanted me, as so far they had only had sons, but my mother was never very interested in babies; she preferred toddlers. Anyway, my early childhood was mainly run by Nanny — so much so that one day when I was about eight I asked her anxiously if it mattered that I seemed to love her more than Mummy. I cannot remember her reply so I suppose it must have been satisfactory. Probably I did not really love either of them much. I tolerated Nanny's billing and cooing over me when she tucked me up in bed at night and dutifully responded to her kisses, but screamed during lesson times with her and, when we went shopping, would walk several paces behind her most of the time, thinking my own thoughts.

Shortly after I was born Keith and Peter, my brothers, were told there was a present for them behind the drawing-room screen. They expected to find a Hornby train; instead they found me. However Keith (five to six years my senior) must have soon forgiven his new-born sister for being such an unwelcome substitute: not long afterwards he saved my life by dislodging a cat from my face where it had settled as I lay in my pram in the garden. Strangely perhaps, I have loved cats all my life (despite some over-'playfulness' with a few of our kittens when I was very young and bored). I bought a kitten for twopence for Peter's ninth birthday. She was a tabby named Fifi after the Weston-super-Mare lifeboat, near which she was born. She remained our family cat, bearing litter after litter of kittens, throughout my childhood. My first career ambition was to run a cattery in partnership with Peter and Nanny. My first published work, written when I was eight, was the following letter to my father's parish magazine (later reprinted in the local Weston-super-Mare paper):

Dear people,
We have got a cat and she's got a kitten called 'Mittens,' and I am asking if any of you could adopt her. We think she is female. We can't keep her because we've got two cats already.
She is a tabby kitten with a white breast and paws and a large forehead which shows she has a lot of brain. If none of you will have her Mummy may have to drown her, so I hope some one will have her.
Love from Pat Arrowsmith

(Mittens in fact did find a home — unlike many of our other less fortunate kittens who went to an untimely, watery grave.)

I was a solemn infant, I'm told, wont to stare fixedly up at people. My grandmother thought I was retarded — but then she thought Keith, a large headed baby, had water on the brain. (He later went to university, became an army major then a government official.) Peter was the lucky baby. One day when he had wind he grinned broadly up at a great-aunt. She, not realising what had prompted the beatific smile, left him £100 in her will.
My earliest recollection is of trying to prop up a broken-legged, toy, pink, tin pig against a miniature birds' house. I was two, I think, at the time. And round about then I

remember playing with a beautiful, big, glass, rainbowed marble — something I would still treasure. My next clear recollection is of being introduced by my vicar's-wife mother to the assembled ladies at one of our church 'working parties' (sewing meetings).

'She's three and a half,' my mother proudly announced.

My father wanted me to be called 'Rebel' as he had seen a picture of a pretty little girl of that name. The local reporters were so surprised to hear this that my mother said it wouldn't do, and the paper incorrectly stated that I was 'Rosemary'. In the end my parents compromised and I was christened (by two bishops — although one arrived late) 'Pat' (without the 'ricia') instead. I am also 'Margaret', after my mother, but never use the name except for such things as bank accounts and driving licences. Not that I knew my real name for a while. When, as a toddler, I was asked by members of my father's parish what I was called I was apt to reply gruffly:

'Little Baby Turtle-Dove,' or 'Little Bundle of Rubbish'.

Red was (and is) my favourite colour, and my fourth birthday was a 'red birthday': all, or most, of my presents were red, so was the shell of my special breakfast boiled egg. And I was certainly no older than four (I can remember the vicarage nursery where this conversation took place) when, watching my mother do up parcels of old clothes, I asked to whom she was sending them. 'To the Jews,' she replied (it was 1933 or '34), whereupon I expressed surprise and said this was impossible since the Jews, being Biblical characters like Angels, must, like them, all be living in Heaven. Even at four I knew you couldn't send parcels of old clothes to Heaven. All the same, for a very long time I believed in Father Christmas and that my teddy-bear, Billy Boy, was alive. He wrote me letters when we went away for the summer holidays, and once his mother — looking suspiciously like one of Peter's teddies with a few additional whiskers stitched on — came to visit me. And he had a home — a hut built (although I didn't know it) by my brothers in the woods at the top of the cliff above our vicarage. When Nanny took me to visit it I usually found awaiting me there a jar of honey, and once a tin of pilchards. But when I started to expect expensive, non-eatable gifts, like three-colour torches, I was disappointed. Incredulity must have begun to set in when I was about eight (probably at about the same time that my mother explained the extraordinary, till then taboo, subject of micturation). Father Christmas was in any case rather like God, with his alleged right to decide who was and who was not worthy of gifts/rewards; and it was not until I was in my early teens that I began seriously to conjecture about God.

My chapter in *Multicolour* (my second novel, written when I was eighteen and had just left school) about Jelly, an imaginary small boy of six, contains many autobiographical elements. I, like Jelly, found Sundays and church-going insufferably boring. Peter and I used to sing 'Onward Christian Soldiers' lustily when others were singing the 'Te Deum' — I quite unaware that we were not all singing the same thing. The description of Jelly's eating difficulties exactly reflects mine as a child of about that age — I spent hours on end over (to me) unappetizing, rapidly congealing midday meals, either being mildly punished for not being able to down the food or, like Jelly, being cajoled by games into eating it. Although a fat child, I had problems over eating my dinner until, years later, I went to boarding school.

The games my brothers and I played on Sunday had all to be suffused with religion. And one wet Sunday we acted out the expulsion from the Marriage Feast — with dire consequences. Although Jelly's tragically culminating adventure in the woods is pure fiction (albeit I was apparently, as a four-year-old, all but abducted by a strange man), my account of it does describe some of my own childhood fantasies and fears, and is, of course, partly about Billy Boy's 'home' in the woods above our vicarage.

'Jelly' (a chapter from *Multicolour*)

Jelly did not like Sundays. An extra cake for tea, provided he ate plain bread and butter first, was not sufficient recompense for the tedium of the day. Sundays were full of don'ts and can'ts.

It rained one Sunday, and Jelly's spirits, which fluctuated with the weather, sank...

After breakfast it was nearly time for Church, but not quite. The interval was too short in which to do anything properly, but too long to be spent doing nothing. Jelly ran about and became hot and dishevelled so that Nanny began to scold again.

Just as they were all about to set off for Church Nanny decided his shoes were dirty. Mosey [mother] tried to persuade her that they would 'do', but Nanny was firm. Jelly was hurried into the pantry and wrenched from his shoes, which Nanny proceeded to brush fiercely. And then they had to hurry so as not to be late...

Church bored Jelly. For Christmas he had been given 'A Little Picture Hymn Book.' He always took it to Church, not realizing that it differed from the books that the others used. But he was learning to read, and was sometimes puzzled and bothered because the words in his book did not seem to correspond at all with those being sung.

This Sunday he decided to sing hymns he knew, and so, while the others were in the midst of the 'Te Deum' he sang 'Gentle Jesus' lustily and almost aggressively. He went on singing it even after several flustered 'quietly nows' from Mosey. Only when he caught a threatening glance from Nanny, and remembered that there were ginger-snaps for tea, did he stop. Instead he considered the seats [buttocks] of the people in front of him. He often did this, and wondered whether the broad middle-aged female seats were twice or three times the size of their comparatively lean and contracted male counterparts. Today there were no interesting seats in view. He turned round to see if there were any behind, and then realized that he could only see people's fronts from that position. He turned back again. He began to pick his nails until he caught another threatening glance from Nanny.

The sermon was the dullest part of the service. Jelly scratched faces on his thigh, and then began a brief pinching match with Pauline, until Denise quietly moved over and sat between them. He gazed at the stained glass windows. There was one in which a group of trees in the background were so clustered as to resemble a gigantic four-foot beast. For many a long five minutes Jelly had stared at this window and wondered whether perhaps the cluster really were a monstrous creature and not just trees. He was much more intrigued by this part of the window than by the group of enigmatic and anaemic saints portrayed in the foreground.

Fortunately it was raining too hard after Church that day for Mosey to stop in the Churchyard and have her usual dull conversations. They hurried home.

Even Sunday dinner was unappetizing. Breakfast was late on Sundays, and dinner more punctual than usual, so that Jelly could still feel breakfast inside him at dinner-time and had no appetite. Sunday dinner was the worst dinner of the week because it was always cold meat and salad. Mosey cooked as little as possible on Sundays. Jelly hated meat, especially cold meat, which was edged with lardy white fat, that he was not allowed to leave, and had no gravy to help it down. Nor did he like salad. He was unable to forget the occasion when he had found two slugs on his lettuce. The watery sweetness of beetroot did not go well with meat. It was junket for pudding. Jelly detested junket. It was not a liquid and yet not a solid food, and it slid down the throat like a soft slippery creature...

Usually most of a Sunday afternoon was spent at Sunday School, but today there was no Sunday School, as it had closed down temporarily. What was there to do? Jelly sometimes found it hard to know what to do on weekdays as he had done everything so often and could not always think out any fresh games. On Sundays it was doubly difficult because everything had to have a religious flavour. Purely secular activities like going for a picnic, going on the beach, listening to 'Children's Hour,' being told a story or playing everyday games in the garden, were forbidden. Special toys were kept for Sundays.

The Children just then had a 'marbles craze'. But marbles were not included among the Sunday Toys, which were mainly composed of quiet Sunday games and pictures of Biblical scenes to colour. Nobody wanted to play with Sunday Toys. Pauline begged in vain to play marbles. In the end they played 'Bible Lexicon' for a while. Jelly, who could not spell properly, 'helped' The Hump [older brother]. They could not play lexicon in the normal fashion on Sundays, but were allowed to play if they chose their words from the Bible. It was a subtle way of forcing them to read the Scriptures. Later someone asked if they might play 'Bible and Prayer Book Lexicon'. Permission was given, but when they asked whether they might choose words from the Angel's [one of the older daughters] 'Helps to Study the Bible', and finally from any religious book, they were forbidden to play the game any longer.

They wracked their brains to think of some other enjoyable, yet suitably sabbatical game. Hilary finally suggested acting Bible scenes. Nanny was upstairs with the Chit [the baby], and so they were able, unchallenged, to derange the Nurseries' furniture, turn the table upside down, and make it into a house by spreading the tablecloth over the legs. They decided to act the Marriage Feast. Jelly was chosen to be the guest without a wedding garment who had to be expelled from the feast. They expelled him roughly and Hilary scratched him by mistake. That was too much. Everything had gone wrong all day and now Hilary had scratched him. Jelly cried with anger and punched her in the tummy... She began to cry... Everybody started to punch... There were no ginger-snaps for tea.

After tea it stopped raining and the sun shone. Jelly wanted to go out. Since Nanny would soon be putting The Chit to bed and the Grown-Ups would be going to Church again he knew there was no chance of his being taken for a walk. Suddenly he decided to go out by himself. He would go and hunt for Fairyland.

Fairyland was a real place for Jelly, and he knew where it was. It was somewhere up in The Woods, in the dense part off the beaten track where they never penetrated. Fairyland and Heaven were almost indistinguishable in his mind. They were both gleaming silver cities full of fruit trees, where there were beautiful women with wings, shining dresses, and magic wands or harps. The only salient difference was that whereas God, the ruler of Heaven, was a man, a queen reigned in Fairyland.

Just outside Fairyland there was a country peopled by live teddy-bears and gollywogs. Jelly knew this because there was a certain foliage covered hut made of twisted branches in The Woods, which, so Nanny told him, was Bruno's parent's home. Bruno was his favourite teddy-bear. He might not have believed Nanny had he not received letters, while he was away in the summer, from Bruno who was left at home. Furthermore, whenever he went to Bruno's house he always discovered a small jar of honey there.

Nanny's fairy-stories afforded Jelly his knowledge of Fairyland and teddy-bear-land. Usually witches and an ogre figured in Nanny's tales, and so Jelly was sure that somewhere in the depths of The Woods there were witche's caves and an ogre's castle. The idea fascinated rather than frightened him. He never felt absolutely certain about it all, but this enhanced the mysterious attraction of The Woods.

He knew that to go out on his own was one of the naughtiest things he could do, and that if he were found out he would be spanked hard. He waited for a little while after tea until Nanny had gone upstairs to see to The Chit. He would have liked Pauline's company but did not ask her to go with him for fear she refused and told Nanny. And so he slipped off unobtrusively without telling anybody. He did not consider how long he might be and that his absence would soon be noticed.

The Woods were not very far away. Nanny took The Children for walks in them occasionally — although not often enough to prevent such walks being 'treats.' Jelly found his way there quite easily.

He ran along the familiar paths until he reached Bruno's house. As usual Bruno's parents were out, but this time there was no note of apology to explain why, as there had always before been, nor, after a long search, did Jelly find a jar of honey. He was disappointed and a trifle surprised. A recent storm had evidently made part of the hut collapse, and Jelly was even more surprised that Bruno's parents had not bothered to repair it. They would have done so in one of Nanny's stories.

After he left Bruno's house Jelly penetrated deeper into The Woods along small winding paths fringed with wet trailing brambles. He felt very excited. At last he could really start to hunt for Fairyland, the ogre's castle, and the witches' caves. He rambled hither and thither forgetful of time. He was happy, although he would have enjoyed the adventure still more had Pauline been there to share it.

He found a small cave, which was more an enlarged crevice than a cave, among some boulders. He wondered whether a very small witch lived there, and then, to his delight, he found close by the ashes of a camp fire. This proved that a witch lived there. Later he found some deep pits which almost turned into tunnels. He scrambled down into one of them but found nothing that betokened an inhabitant. But that was no proof that no one lived there...

Later he reached a rocky stream, and he realized that this was the boundary over which he must cross to find the ogre's castle, witches' caves and Fairyland. But he did not find them. He searched for a long time and he searched continuously, without stopping to swing on branches or try to climb trees. He grew tired, and gradually began to wonder whether Fairyland were in this wood at all. There were many other woods where it might equally well be... Perhaps after all there was no Fairyland...

Presently he discovered blackberries. There were no black-berries in the familiar part of The Woods. He picked fistfuls and crammed them into his mouth. He forgot about Fairy-land.

Sometime later he decided he had eaten enough blackber-ries and would go home. He could look for Fairyland another day when perhaps Pauline was with him.

And then he noticed that the leaves were no longer glittering with sunshine. It was growing dark. He realized that he must have been out a very long time, perhaps an hour or two, and that Nanny would have found out. He would be spanked. Soon he stopped worrying about being spanked because he realized he was lost. All the narrow twisting paths he followed joined others equally narrow instead of a broad familiar one. He could not even find the stream again. It grew darker. The dampness of the undergrowth made the bramble scratches on his legs sting. He was cold.

All at once he was frightened. He started to run. Everything in The Woods behind started to run after him. He did not know whither he was running nor why. The ogre, witches and hordes of goblins and demons were chasing him... He could almost hear the ogre crashing through the undergrowth and the witches hissing through the air... Logs and boulders reared themselves up in his path. Branches tugged him back. Brambles clawed at his legs... He stumbled. He slipped in puddles. He tripped over stones and fell. He picked himself up and ran on...

Suddenly he heard an ordinary man's voice. Immediately the witches, ogre, and goblins became unreal and he was terrified no longer. Soon he was sobbing hysterically into the coat of the strange man, who was comforting him. It did not occur to Jelly, against whom all the terrors of the supernatural had just been unleashed, to fear the man. Although rough voiced and raggedly dressed, he seemed kind. He offered to take Jelly home. They walked on.

Presently they arrived at a small hut, which Jelly had never seen before. The man said it was where he was living for the moment, and took Jelly in to give him some food. When they were inside he told Jelly to sit on a box, and brought him a wedge of bread and cheese.

Until then he had not ceased to talk to Jelly, but now he became silent. Jelly did not notice this until he had finished eating, and then he became aware of the man's eyes staring at him. Before, his face had seemed quite ordinary and pleasant, but suddenly Jelly thought it looked rather queer. The eyes were burning. He was looking at him in an odd frightening way that Jelly did not understand. He knelt close beside Jelly, put his arm round his neck and stroked his throat. And then Jelly understood. This was the ogre. He struggled to free himself... The hands gripped about his neck. The thumbs pressed into his throat... He struggled until he could struggle no more.

They found his body next day.

* * *

Although I cannot recall precisely such an incident ever occurring in the woods behind our house, they were at one time supposed to harbour a 'mad' dentist — for whom my father was once mistaken when out on one of his regular evening runs (jogging anticipated by decades). And my brothers' schoolmates once found a man hanging dead from a tree there — presumably a suicide.

2

My parents were exceedingly religious, if not precisely spiritual — particularly in my father's case. He was descended from more than one 'hot-gospeller' and was a 'low' Church of England parson who believed in Sin and Salvation.

My mother's Plymouth Brethren missionary parents and sister had all been stoned to death by mistake in China when my mother was two. (They were thought to be Roman Catholics, against whom there was a local vendetta, and didn't get out of town in time. My mother survived by being hidden under a bed and drugged into silence by her Chinese nurse.) I 'came to Jesus' (was 'born again') a number of times as I was apt to fear the conversion had not worked properly. Peter 'came' when he was four. Aware that this was quite a youthful feat, he wondered at the time whether the fact would be recorded in some celestial version of *The Guinness Book of Records*. As young children, we all prayed aloud at our mother's knee. In addition to making the standard 'God bless Mummy, Daddy, Gran, Brothers, Nanny, Maids... etc.' string of requests, we had also to pray for remote, underprivileged groups — in my brothers' case, The Unemployed; in mine, The Outcasts. Eventually I found there were so many requests I wanted to make of God which I didn't want the grown-ups to know about that I asked if I might pray privately. My mother seemed surprised and saddened.

Although I was superficially a rumbustuous little girl, decidedly quarrelsome and apt to yell loudly at Nanny, I was at the same time quite a frightened, conscience-stricken child. I had eating difficulties; I was afraid of the dark when in bed at night, frightened of wolves, ghosts, the house blowing over, and (later) of being kidnapped — so much so that whenever something ghoulish began to feature in a family conversation my brothers would murmur warningly, 'Heads, stones and corpses,' in order to get the subject changed.

When I was seven or eight I went through a period of dreading going to bed at night because of nightmares. And there was a phase when I would cling onto my sheet in bed to prevent myself sleep-walking (which in fact I did only once, and then only to the other end of my bed where I awoke shivering to be comforted by Nanny, whose bedroom I shared). I worried endlessly too about whether I would go to Heaven or Hell when I died (this probably prompted by the heavy doses of religion we received form our parents). For a time I irritatingly followed almost every statement I made with 'perhaps', just in case, unwittingly, I had not told the absolute truth hence would be damned. For the same reason I had to ask to be forgiven for my every slightest misdeed.

Hilary in *Multicolour*, quite unlike me at that age in many ways, nevertheless reflects a significant side of my nature as a young child.

'Hilary' (a chapter from *Multicolour*)

Hilary knew that she did not really count. It may have been because she was squeezed so closely between The Hump and Pauline that nobody properly noticed her...

'Humphrey you can come — oh and Hilary might as well...' or:

'Pauline, lamb, you wait here with me — and Hilary you had

better too.' She was an afterthought.

Many things frightened Hilary, perhaps because of her feeling of inferiority, or perhaps as the cause. She found most of the other members of the family alarming...

It was not only people that made her afraid. Sometimes when they were away in the summer she had a bedroom to herself. If she did not fall asleep before the landing light was switched off, she could scarcely close her eyes for terror because there was utter darkness, and even the one ray of light under the door that betokened a world of mortals without, had been obliterated.

The summer holidays were three quarters spoilt because she was frightened of the sea. There might be a tidal wave... But she could never tell anyone, because, if she did, another even greater fear, that of being laughed at, would be realized. And so whenever they went in caves she had to try to force herself to forget that something might crash in and block up the entrance so that they were trapped... And when they were on a precarious ledge halfway up a cliff she could never look down, but had to say quickly over and over to herself:

'We are on the back lawn at home, we are on the back lawn at home...' Once The Angel had said:

'What the Hell are you muttering about Hilary? What's wrong now?' It had been alright. She had not guessed.

She forced herself to bathe when they were away on holiday. She even made herself stay in with The Hump long after the others were out so that no one might guess... Just once she had been right under the water when the rubber dinghy capsized... They had all been very surprised when she had re-appeared and promptly started to sob hysterically. Nobody realized how delighted she was one year when it was to be an inland holiday, nor her disappointment when she heard that they would be close by a lake and so able to bathe every day. The grown-ups, except for Father and Gil, used from time to time to be 'off bathing' for a day or two. Everyone was so used to this, except in the case of The Angel, that usually no questions were asked. One day, when the sea looked especially frothy and pugnacious, Hilary thought she too would be 'off bathing.' They all looked at her in amazement and then burst out laughing.

Over and above her own private fears Hilary suffered on account of others. The calves of her legs twitched with nervousness while Gil read the lesson in Church for the first time. Sometimes she was on tenterhooks lest Pauline should be rude and cause a scene. When Pauline was spanked she had to strain her ears to hear, through the screams, when it stopped. This was not sadistic curiosity, but because, until she knew it was over, she could almost feel the blows on herself. Sometimes, when The Hump was not there, Pauline and Jelly would catch grasshoppers and tear off there legs. When they did this she always went away and read in order to try to forget what was happening. If she could not divert her mind she almost became one of the grasshoppers and could very nearly feel a wrenching at her own thigh-bone socket. She never punished her teddy-bears or ripped off their ears as Pauline did...

Nearly everything in life was rather spoilt for Hilary because of her fear. Unpleasantness seemed doubly unpleasant when peppered by fear. When everything was going well she was afraid it would all be spoilt. When she was with people she liked and admired she felt nervous in case she were boring them. There were so many things that should have been fun, and which everyone else enjoyed, which were spoilt for her because they made her afraid...

The winter that she was nine Hilary caught a bad chill. She was glad that it was a chill and not something infectious, for, had it been the latter, the others would probably have caught it too. She would not then have been 'poor little Hilary, who's got such a nasty chill.' She would just have been 'one of The Children down with measles.' But, as she was the only invalid, she seemed to acquire more individuality than was normally hers. She became someone special and set apart, who had to have separate trays and with whom They had to 'be careful' because she was 'not very strong.'...

But there was also much that was unpleasant about being ill. When she was feeling too ill or weary to read or colour pictures, and when no one was there talking to her or reading aloud, she thought about herself being ill. This made her start to wonder about dying. Did it hurt very much? Would she gasp for breath until she could gasp no more? Or would she 'peacefully pass away with a little smile hovering about the lips,' an adoring family gathered around, and church bells softly pealing from away over the hills in the sunset as children in books did? Hilary felt that it was not so easy and peaceful and that 'little smiles' did not 'hover'. She imagined her face becoming blackened and distorted as she tried in vain to breathe, unable to raise her voice to call for the others... She could almost feel her breath beginning to come gaspingly...

Inevitably, thinking about dying made her start to worry about what happened afterwards. She forgot about gasping for breath, and began to wonder whether there really were Heaven or Hell. She knew quite well that Heaven was not merely a place of substantial clouds and tinkling harps, nor had it been impressed on her since infancy that wicked people, when they died, were relegated to a flaming pit. Her ideas of Heaven and Hell were vague and unformulated. Heaven was just somewhere where Christians went when they died and where everything was alright for ever. Hell was for the rest and was a place of eternal agony, none the less so because it was not a fiery pit.

As she lay in bed, awful ideas sidled into Hilary's mind. Would there, after all, be anything more when she had died? If not, would she become just nothing? and if so, what was it like to be nothing? And 'for ever and ever' — even if everything were alright 'for ever and ever,' surely it must end sometime? Perhaps everything, Heaven, the stars and universe, all the souls and angels, and even God, would end sometime... But what then?... And the universe, where did that end too? Were there many universes, one inside another, like lots of balls inside each other? But then outside the outside one?...

Such speculations became too much to cope with, and her mind returned to the more particular. She herself, was she 'saved', or would she be one of those sent off to Hell? She had already been 'saved' once or twice. The first time was at a terrifying beach service, but, a month or two later, she felt it could not have worked, as she had done so many bad things since. She then had to do something very hard, go and tell Father about it. He was very kind, and she 'came to Jesus' again. But every time afterwards that she did something wrong, she had to 'come to Jesus' again on her own, and every time it seemed less and less real. It was very difficult. When-ever she was even a little naughty, and she never was very, she had to ask Them to forgive her, as it did not count only to ask God — that was too easy. And she had to confess any slightly bad deed that They did not know of. To begin with They were sympathetic and took it all seriously, but, as time went on, They became rather off-hand and short with her and did not listen properly. Pauline, Jelly and The Angel, when they knew about it, teased her mercilessly from time to time.

Death was possibly imminent, and Hilary, as she lay in bed and thought, became even more worried than when she was well, about Hell, whether she were 'saved' or not, and whether she had confessed and been forgiven all her bad deeds. What was Hell like? Did people go there for always, or might they be let out after, say, ten thousand years? Had she told about that cup she had cracked? and the time when she had argued back with Pauline and got cross? If not she must do so quickly before it were too late. And so she felt quite ill and heavy inside until They came and she was able to bring herself to tell. Father was sent for, and she 'came to Jesus' all over again. She could not feel really safe, and as though her rooms in Heaven were properly booked, until she had. That evening her temperature was up.

She was afraid of going to sleep too because of the nightmares she had. When she was younger, she had been afraid to go to bed because of the bad dreams from which she had suffered—dreams about ghosts, crooked-fingered witches, and houses blowing over. Once the ghost had been Father, a terrible Father with glazed and staring eyes... That had been one of the worst dreams. By the time she was nine she had almost grown out of bad dreams, and she quite often forgot when the two-monthly interval of respite was up and she was due for another. Now that she was ill she had bad dreams constantly again. They were different from those of before. They were vague and intangible — something immeasurably huge and heavy and something infinitesimally minute colliding...

Ghosts, perhaps, were more terrifying than anything else. As she was ill, Hilary had been temporally allowed a room to herself. One night they left her door ajar but forgot to leave on the landing light...

What was that blob of light that seemed to flicker about on the ceiling? It was like a shiny half-crown...no, more like an eye staring down at her... Wouldn't it go away? What was it anyway, and why was it there? There wasn't anything to make it be there... How could it be anything to do with the lights outside? If she shut her eyes she could feel it staring down at her. She had to open them... Perhaps it really was an eye...the eye of something dark, shadowy, something of a shape she had never seen before...something...dreadful...

There was a white thing over in the corner by the fire-place. Something white and crouching, almost like a polar-bear. And it had eyes — surely those were eyes. It moved. 'Oh God, please may it not move again, and please make it go away.' She shut her eyes. She opened them. It was still there...but perhaps it was not quite so like a polar-bear after all... Yes, of course, she remembered now — the armchair. Nanny had put it by the fire and hung the extra blanket over it.

But the eye on the ceiling. It must be an eye. Wouldn't it go away? She couldn't sleep with it staring down at her...

What was that creak... Something in the corner over there... What? She had heard it before. Nanny said it was mice in the wainscoting, but wasn't it really the tables and chairs and things settling down for the night? Or was it, perhaps, something else?...

A tap on the window!... A murderer? A burglar? A kidnapper?... No, no, of course not. It had happened before, and Nanny said it was just the ivy blown agains the glass...and yet...somehow it didn't sound like ivy, so perhaps it wasn't and something really was knocking...

Why couldn't she get to sleep? In the morning it would all be alright. Nanny would come and wake her. The eyes and knocks and things would all just seem silly then.

Suddenly she heard it. It could not be anything else this time. She had known all along it would come for her one day. A soft pattering sound in the distance... It was getting nearer, louder...

'Oh God, please. I'm sorry I was rude to Nanny today...so please, please, make it go away'... Nearer...nearer...louder... It pushed open the door... It was there, at her bedside, just by her... It was going to spring at her...

'No! No! Please God no!'...

It sprang. A scream. Silence.

A surge of people. Nanny, Mosey, Denise, Gil... Lights on. They lifted Growler off the bed. He was purring. They found Hilary motionless.

For a day or two she was dangerously ill.

* * *

I myself, when several years older than Hilary at the time of her illness, was still afraid of getting kidnapped from my bed at night — I had read a school-story which had included such an incident. Strangely, however, when Keith returned very late one night from Home Guard and, climbing back in through my bedroom window foolishly pretended to be a wicked intruder, I was not frightened at all. I don't think I can have had time to be — I so soon, fortunately, realised who the intruder was.

Peter (pencil; age fifteen)

Mummy Sewing (pencil/ink; age fifteen)

3

I suppose I was quite an intelligent little girl. My mother used to tell people proudly how I once remarked that the Earth could not go off course because it was fixed in its orbit; and the grown-ups were very impressed when, in the course of some literary game at a children's party, it emerged that I could spell the word 'efficient' correctly. My mother was at a loss once when I told her I could accept such divine miracles as the Feeding of the Five Thousand but was sure there was one thing that even God couldn't do — make yesterday into today. He might be able to make yesterday *seem* just like today, or vice versa, but surely he couldn't make it *actually* today. My mother (not a higher mathematician) was, as far as I can remember, floored, and no doubt prevaricated.

I began to learn to read (with coloured cardboard letters) when I was four — possibly three, and I read my first story-book laboriously in my head I think when I was six and ill in bed. At about the same time I wrote my first essay — on William the Conqueror. The grown-ups were very impressed by it.

I didn't much like being a child. I hated being thought babyish, being petted or smiled at indulgently by my elders, being kissed by my father's parishioners and being teased for being fat. My brothers nicknamed me 'Trunk' or 'Trunky' because of my tubbiness and square build — not my nose, which was quite ordinary. The nickname stuck until I was an adult. (My family were great nicknamers: we all had them. Like me, Keith and Peter were never, as children, called by their real names; and we had quite insulting nicknames for our mother and grandmother. During the war our parents were known jointly as 'The High Command'.)

I longed to grow up, and badly wanted to wake up one morning and find I was twelve.

I had a rather Victorian early childhood. Nanny was quite a young woman who lived with us for years and was, among many other things, my governess until I was nine and she left us to become a hospital nurse. My brothers, being boys, went to local prep schools at the normal age. I was learning French, elementary geometry and vulgar fractions (although I was never good at mathematics) by the time I was eight as I received Nanny's exclusive attention — except for a brief period when another little girl joined us. This somehow made Lessons, which previously I had found mainly difficult (especially arithmetic) and dull, suddenly and surprisingly quite fun. When I could recite my tables to perfection Nanny gave me as a prize a little golden spider on a silver web pendant of hers which I had long coveted — even though I was, and still am, terrified of spiders and daddy-long-legs. Amazingly, I still have it. Like my father I was always, and still am, a great hoarder and retainer of my possessions — the little real roll-top desk, a childhood Christmas present, is still among my furniture. And as a child I was also a great collector: stamps, autographs, pressed flowers, small lead animals... I suppose I still am in a way a collector, but now of less tangible things.

I paid a price for my solo education. As a young child I was rather lonely. Not going to school I did not have friends, and life was monotonous. My brothers, who at that time tended to chum up, leaving me out of things, seemed to have a more interesting time than I; and although I was the Parish darling, and at that time Daddy's pet I suppose, I envied them. My mother, I could tell, preferred them to me: I could hear her reading to them and romping with them in bed. She much less often read to or romped with me after I was tucked up.

My parents' main reason for not sending me to school at the normal age was financial: it was both cheaper and better for Nanny to teach me. Kindergarten pupils at Westcliff, the local girls' private school that comprised a substantial part of my father's church congregation, learned how to make woolly toys, whereas Nanny, infinitely more cheaply, taught me history, nature-study and long division. The Westcliff Deputy Headmistress came to coffee one day when I was about eight and said to me:

'So when will you be coming to Westcliff, Pat?' Without thinking, I instantly and innocently replied:

'I don't know. Mummy and Daddy don't think the education there is good enough.' Then, realising how unwittingly rude I had been, I retired from the room in confusion and confessed to my mother what I had said. Luckily she was wryly amused.

However, although I never became a Westcliff pupil I did attend a weekly junior sort of dancing class there (known as 'rhythmics'). Since for most of the time I was the sole non-pupil to attend I was despised and ostracised hence performed badly and came to dread the weekly ordeal. I took part in some Christmas school concert at which the class danced the 'cat polka' and 'frog in the pool', but I seemed incapable of learning to skip. Afraid that the other girls would laugh at me for my ineptitude, I practised desperately in the garden one day before going to the class. Florence, the family maid (one of the many South Wales girls who came over to posh Somerset at that time to be exploited as domestic servants), who was watching me, commented that I looked 'white with fear'.

During my early years, in Weston-super-Mare, I had one 'friend': Jane, a girl of my age who lived opposite. In due course she went to Westcliff and from then on looked down on me and ignored me at the dancing class. She came over to play daily (she lived in a flat and we had quite a big, interesting vicarage garden) until she went to school; thereafter only on Saturdays. We quarrelled most of the time and managed to enjoy our games usually only on the fairly rare occasions when Peter joined in.

Peter, two to three years older than I, was an imaginative boy. In later years, when Keith was abroad in the army, we became such close friends that people sometimes took us for twins. In early days he hovered between Keith and me. Keith was much livelier and more rough-and-tumble than Peter, who was quiet, almost to the point of being withdrawn, and, unlike Keith, seldom got into trouble. Keith always seemed to have exciting ideas about things to do, and, although when we were quite young we quarrelled a good deal and he was apt to boss me about and give me a walloping, later on he became quite my hero.

Peter and I rarely quarrelled — he wasn't quarrelsome. When he played with me the games (with teddy-bears and the like) came alive. He had whole families and hierarchies of teddy-bears (sometimes armed as mini-soldiers with sticks), while I had Billy Boy, clad immaculately in a suit made by Nanny.

Seaside summer holidays were high spots of the year, for which we all meticulously saved up our few pennies' weekly pocket money for months beforehand. On summer holidays Peter would sometimes take me for delightful walks in the sand dunes. The Hump in *Multicolour* is closely modelled on Peter as a small boy, and the chapter about him illustrates certain aspects of our family summer holidays. Even the incident in which the sand cave collapsed is based on fact: Keith was indeed once nearly killed when a sand cave the three of us had been constructing crumbled down on him. I myself probably came as near death then as on any other occasion in my life. Nanny was sitting knitting and reading close by oblivious of what was going on. Keith was in the cave, which Peter and I were just about to enter, when it collapsed. We alerted Nanny and between us scrabbled Keith out by the hair just in time.

'The Hump' (a chapter from *Multicolour*)

More than anything else in life The Hump enjoyed the summer holidays. It was because They were all there together, and yet he could go off on his own almost whenever he wanted to.

He enjoyed waking up on a summer holiday morning. If it were going to be a hot day, he awoke to find the sunshine sieved through the trelliswork of the trees and playing rippling tunes on the wallpaper. He heard the chewing cows outside wrenching at the grass, and the enticingly mellow calls of roosting wood-pigeons. He could feel that it was the country.

If it were a dull day there might be a film of mist or fine rain over everything. That early morning smell, closely connected with the dampness of early morning grass beneath bare feet, would be stronger than on bright sunny mornings. Everything would be silent and mysterious, and he could still feel that it was the country. One of his pleasantest feelings on awakening on a summer holiday morning was a feeling of exciting uncertainty. Whatever happened today would be fun... but what would happen?

And summer holiday breakfasts were different. They smelt much more savoury than home ones, which could not be smelt at all beforehand, except just near the kitchen. On summer holidays they cooked on an oil stove, which seemed to The Hump much more exciting than the electric one at home. And the frying breakfasty smell was bound up with the oil-stove smell.

After breakfast there was no sinking feeling about 'all the things to be got down to'. He hurried out to the raspberry canes in the garden, which was rambling and terraced, with flights of stone steps, flanked by dark bushy lurking places. If Pauline had arrived there before him, he could usually find some plum trees elsewhere that she had not yet discovered. He enjoyed seeing how much fruit he could collect, and then having a feeling of secret importance later at picnic lunch-time, when he knew he had more plums than the others, which he had picked for himself and hoarded in his pockets. The difficulty about plum picking was that it was forbidden. The only way of circumventing the difficulty, so that he did not tell a lie, was, either to create artificial gales, or else to eat the fruit as it grew, without picking it, leaving the trees dangling with half-naked stones...

The drive to the sea was very exciting. He, Hilary, Pauline, Jelly, and sometimes even The Angel and Gil would have a competition to see who could see the sea first. And if Mosey and Nanny had sufficiently recovered and cooled down, they might even join in too, and then Denise would as well. Sometimes the person who won would be awarded two extra squares of chocolate after lunch. The Hump enjoyed it immensely, even if he did not win. But the real excitement for him was not so much the competition as the actual first glimpsing of the sea, a tantalising blue triangle between the sloping hills. This was the best moment of the day, better even than the first feel of the sea. His excitement was not quite over even when he had seen the sea, because afterwards, as the car descended the hill, the hot, yellow-brown, grass-fringed dunes came into view...

He enjoyed undresssing to bathe. Shoes off first, and no more hot, clogging sand between the toes — just soft, loose sand beneath the feet, to be kicked at Pauline, until someone started to say:

'Children...'

Off with damp clinging shirt. The trouser-trunks exchange was difficult. It did not matter who saw him naked in the bathroom;[1] it was different on the beach. There might be strangers not far off who ought not to see him trouserless. It

[1] When young, surprisingly perhaps, my brothers and I all strip-washed stark naked together in cold water every morning winter and summer — a procedure we called 'morning cold-tub heroes'! My mother was a prude, my father something of a nudist.

was even necessary to be modest before the family on the beach.

After he was undressed and in his bathing-trunks, with the burning sun already beginning to enrich his skin, he watched the others as they strove with tapes and corsets. Nanny undressed Jelly, then seized Pauline and clasped her close to undress her, while Pauline struggled and kept saying:

'Can they see?' The Hump would try to see as much as possible, which was not difficult, just because they were on the beach, and he ought not to. Then it was Hilary's turn. She was thin and pliable in Nanny's hands, and was quite quickly squirmed out of her clothes. But it was funniest to watch the Grown-ups. Nanny and Mosey held up bathing-wraps as screens for one another in turn, and gasped over hooks and pink elastic. Denise was too shy for such a display, and slipped off to the privacy of a dip in the dunes. Once Pauline had followed her secretly and watched. She had been spanked when they arrived home. The Angel too, had recently started to make a fuss about undressing. She had just begun to wash in the bathroom alone with the door bolted. On the beach she made a great show with draped bathing wraps.

They all looked very odd in their bathing costumes. Father, who, dressed, seemed lean and yet quite 'a fine figure of a man', was all nobbly and out of shape in his striped bathing costume. Mosey looked huge and rather like an over-flowing shopping basket. Pauline was just a barrel, and Denise, buxom when dressed, looked much fatter and less compact in a bathing-dress. Gil had a few fascinating hairs on the centre of his chest. The Hump would very much have liked to have had hairs on his chest too. Nanny no longer looked fierce and tyrannical, but seemed cringing and almost embarrassed, as though she wanted, as soon as possible, to hasten into the sea to hide.

For The Hump there was no place on earth where he could have such complete freedom as in the sea. But, before he got there, there were a few moments of delicious anticipation as he bounded across the wet blue sand, leaving pale, quickly-vanishing imprints as he ran. The sand became furrowed as he approached the sea, and he splashed through little troughs of lukewarm water. Finally he was there. Threads of sunlight, like yellow cotton, intertwined on the rippled sand beneath the water. He kicked up fountains of spray and flung himself at the waves in happy abandonment.

Sometimes The Hump played with the others. They made forts and boats, and saw whose castle could longest withstand the incoming tide. From time to time they ran into the sea and splashed about. They might scramble over the rocks for awhile and fish in the pools with their hands for little transparent jellyish fish. Every so often they ran up to the beach shop to spend some of their savings on ice-creams or 'Mars Bars'.[2]

The others liked The Hump to play with them because he was good at playing. They did not squabble so much when he was with them. The forts seemed real forts, and sometimes they actually caught one or two fish. They hardly ever did when he was not with them, as Jelly complained about the rocks scratching his feet, and they would have to return to the sands.

But The Hump liked most to be able to wander off on his own. He could think about pirates and treasure-filled caves much better if he scrambled over the rocks by himself. He could stare into the clear green pools and wonder whether the seaweedy edges were vast forests, and the sea-anemones greedy ogres to the fish swimming about at the bottom, much better when he as alone, than when the others were saying:

'Come on...'

It was Hilary especially who wanted to be with him. Pauline had Nanny and Jelly with whom to bicker, but Hilary was

---

[2] When I was a toddler Keith took me off, as a joke, to 'buy' sweets at the beach shop with a wooden 'penny' (some wooden disk he had found). The shopkeeper I believe was amused — but not my parents: this had been tantamount to stealing...

slightly older than her. Occasionally she asked, almost shyly, if she might stroll off with The Hump. He did not mind her company sometimes, because she did not talk too much, and, when she did talk, it was usually in the right way when they were alone together. She was similar to him in some ways.

One day, as The Hump and Hilary walked together along the sands, hunting for odd-shaped shells and seagulls' skeletons, they came to a place where the firm damp part of the sands sloped rather steeply down to the edge of the sea, and made a kind of bank. They were both carrying their spades. At once the idea of hollowing out a cave occurred to The Hump. With a cave of their own they could play smugglers properly, and perhaps even hide in it from the others, and stay down and spend the night... So they dug away happily and silently until there was quite a roomy cave. The Hump, as eldest and chief architect, went in first to survey. Hilary was about to follow him, when suddenly the roof crumbled in, and there was no more cave — and no more Hump.

It was all so sudden and so soon over that The Hump could scarcely recall afterwards what it had felt like. There was hardly long enough for him to think about not being able to breathe or move. But Hilary never forgot. She experienced an instant's shock and feeling of utter paralysis, and then made a wild scrabble in the sand until she unearthed a tuft of hair and gradually wrenched The Hump to light. Fortunately, the cave had not been very large, and The Hump had not been buried beneath too mountainous a heap of sand. The experience was one of the unpleasant ones that The Hump did not think about much afterwards. Hilary did. She added the horror of it to the accumulation of fears and terrors that made her a timid child. She also remembered the incident with faint pride, because it was she who had saved The Hump's life...

They went back to tea with the others. Afterwards there was serf-board sliding on the dunes, and then the journey back. Presently it was bed-time. It was wiser for Nanny and Mosey not to know what had happened, and so they did not tell the others about the cave.

4

Nanny was an excellent dress-maker and made me beautifully smocked frocks that I hated because, minus waistlines, they made me feel fat and babyish and conspicuously unlike other little girls in properly shaped dresses.

I had other toy animals as well as Billy Boy (who was possibly loved more by Nanny than by me). I had dolls too (which I did not particularly want at first) because, as a little girl, I was supposed to have them. I brushed their china heads dutifully every morning and deplored Jane's laziness in leaving hers all day in their nighties in their toy cots. On the whole I preferred boys' toys to girls' — perhaps because I tried to model myself on my brothers — and was sometimes given them. For my sixth birthday I received a pop-gun, torch and tin sword. I had the temerity to pursue some cows with drawn sword until one of them turned round and glared balefully at me. When I was eight I was actually allowed to have a real, splendid, big, red-handled, multi-bladed and gadgeted knife.

Pauline is, perhaps, the most directly autobiographical character in *Multicolour*. The account of her eighth birthday (birthdays were another of the year's highlights) is, like the rest of *Multicolour*, fiction; but it contains many truths, and, among other things, reflects a certain aspect of my feelings and attitude towards my father at that age.

The spanking which rounded off the day's events was like the periodic spankings and canings I myself received (Keith was frequently birched unmercifully). Undoubtedly my father had a sadistic streak. He frequently extolled the merits of corporal punishment, quoting 'spare the rod and spoil the child' to back his case. And his occasional bedtime reading to me was his *Naughtinesses*, a sort of modernised, doggerel version of *Struwelpeter* (soft porn in fact) in which the 'naughty' child victim usually received graphically described (and illustrated) corporal punishment. These fables undoubtedly awakened some erotic feelings in me (of course unrecognised as such) although the actual dreaded spankings certainly didn't. However, when my father (who kept the cane he used conspicuously displayed on his study bookshelf) actually did inflict corporal punishment on me I could hardly fail to realise that, despite all the preliminary 'This hurts me more than it hurts you dear' utterances, he actually rather enjoyed doing it. How could it be otherwise in view of his *Naughtinesses*, written with such gusto and read cloyingly to me in bed or seated on his knee.

'Pauline' (a chapter from *Multicolour*)

Pauline had a boom and slump temperament. When she was pleased or happy she was overpoweringly — so much so that almost inevitably reaction set in and suddenly life was utterly miserable and not worth living.

Pauline grew up without a true sense of proportion. If she wanted something she went on wanting it badly, regardless of what people said, even when perhaps she herself realized underneath that she ought not to have it. If she were miserable, everything in life turned several shades darker, and all the good things seemed to be good from some ulterior motive. When something pleasant happened, it was wonderful, not just pleasant, and everything else was wonderful too.

Even her eighth birthday was a day of booms and slumps.

It had been hard to fall asleep the night before, because she could not stop thinking about all that was going to happen next day, and the presents she was going to have. She was so excited that she was still awake at nine o'clock. Then she suddenly began to grow worried because she would never be seven again. It was all over, and she had lost all the chances she had not taken when she was seven... Nothing, not even God, could make her seven again...but God could do anything, so they told her. Had she not been praying for a sheath-knife with a goat's foot handle for weeks and weeks?... It was very puzzling, because she knew God ought to be able to do anything, and yet at the same time she knew quite well that he could not make her seven again. He could tip all the stars into the Atlantic Ocean. He could make all the things that had happened while she was seven happen again in just the same way, but he just could not make her actually seven again, she knew he could not.

She became worried, and then a little frightened. It was late and dark and perhaps God would strike her dead or send bears to maul her in bed for doubting his power. She began to call for Mosey and Nanny alternately, but when they came they did not seem able to understand or put things right. She stopped being frightened and began to feel slightly cross. They sent for Father. They would not have had she been Hilary, The Hump or one of the others, but she was Father's favourite. It was because she was talkative, bouncy, chubby and naughty — all the things Father had never been. Father seemed almost to understand. He was calm, like The Hump, and not fussy and noisy like Mosey. He succeeded in imbuing her with some of his calmness, and made Nanny fetch her some cocoa. After that she soon went to sleep.

She awoke very early, and, of course, could not stay in bed. It was her birthday. She plunged into Nanny's room and woke up The Chit, who began to cry, and Jelly, with whom she started a pillow fight. Then Nanny awoke. She had forgotten about it being a birthday, and was early-morningish because

The Chit was crying. Pauline did not care. She and Jelly ran away, bounced in on Hilary, and woke her up with a start by pulling her hair. Hilary's dreams rapidly resolved themselves into a nightmare, at the climax of which she awoke terrified. When she had recovered enough to be cross, she and Pauline began a real fight. The Angel was woken by the noise, and came in and refereed the battle with gusto. Gil, also woken, thought he had better 'go and see what all the racket was in aid of'. So did Denise. They both started to try to still the uproar, and then began to argue as to which of them was in authority.

Nanny, the screeching Chit in arms, was just arriving to increase the tumult in attempts to quell it, and Pauline was just beginning to feel furious with everyone, when Father appeared. The noise died down, the throng gradually disbanded, and Pauline was borne off to Father's and Mosey's bed.

She was too wide awake to think of sleep any more, and anyway Father wanted to play with her, although Mosey was still comatose and did not much want him to. They played 'nose pinching' and 'down falls the mountain', Pauline seated on Father's crooked knees which he would suddenly relax. Presently she began to feel quieter, and sat still until it was time to get up.

She felt very pleased and important at breakfast-time. Everyone, even Nanny and The Chit, went into the dining-room with the Grown-ups for breakfast on a birthday. She had grapes and fried egg and bacon while the others from 'The Nurseries' only had corn flakes and bread and butter and marmalade. There were presents all round her plate, and, in the middle of the table, was her cake, a hurriedly finished off creation of Mosey's but good to eat, and gaily iced, which pleased Pauline...

There was a good pile of presents because it was a big family, and, besides the family, there were relations and godmothers, and all the elderly couples in the parish who sent presents to her, although they did not to the others, because she looked 'so sweet.' There were books about schoolgirls who trapped German spies. There were chocolates. There were dull things like hankeys from godmothers. Aunty Chummy sent her a dress. Pauline was annoyed about this because it was not really a present to her at all, but one to Nanny and Mosey. Aunty Chummy must have known this too because she had slipped in some chocolates as well. Pauline was also annoyed because Uncle Terry always sent her money, and this time there was a china doll from 'Nanny and Uncle Terry.' Just for an instant she wondered at this strange combination of donors, and then she understood. They had kept trying to make her want dolls because they did not like her to be boyish and want sheath-knives and pistols, so they had bought this doll with Uncle Terry's money, and Nanny had dressed it. For weeks past Nanny had been unusually vague, and the others had grinned in a funny way, whenever she had suggested that The Chit was a bit big for the dress Nanny was making. There was a Prayer Book from Granny. Pauline had one already.

There were also some presents that she liked very much. Father gave her a fascinating torch that could shine yellow, red or green. Mosey gave her the little toy tin typewriter at which she had so often gazed longingly in Webster's. Jelly, Hilary and The Hump gave her a knife. It was quite big, but only a penknife because it opened and shut. She wondered how much it had cost, because that made so much difference. She was afraid it must have been cheap, partly because they could not have afforded anything very expensive, and partly because there was a little scratch on the wooden looking handle that revealed tinny metal underneath. Gil gave her a Margaret Tarrant picture because he thought it was a suitable sort of picture to hang in a little girl's bedroom. Pauline liked it because there were no fairies in it, as in most of Margaret Tarrant's paintings, but only a girl and boy lolling on rocks by the sea. Denise gave her the new pencil-case that she wanted, and The Angel gave her a red plastic purse. There was money from a few people.

But there was no sheath-knife with a goat's foot handle.

Pauline had been craving for one ever since the summer when she had seen one attached to the belt of a Boy Scout. They had all laughed at her, but she had remained firmly insistent that this was what she wanted most. Always before she had been given all she wanted on her birthday, and she had never before wanted anything so badly as to be able to fix a really big, fierce, boyish knife on to her belt. Everything was spoilt.

Pauline was not unkind, and she did her best not to let the others see how spoilt everything was. Hilary saw instantly, and knew why. She did not say anything, but she was terrified lest the others should see too and be hurt, and lest there should be a scene. She had realized all along how much Pauline had longed for a goat's foot handled knife. Hilary had not dared to say much about it, except to The Hump, who had agreed to club together with her, adding on Jelly's sixpence, in order to buy the best possible substitute for the coveted knife.

There was so much clearing up to be done of breakfast things and parcel débris, and Jelly jumped about so much, telling Pauline how lovely all her presents were, that nobody else noticed her disappointment. Mosey and Nanny agreed together afterwards that Pauline had not seemed quite so thrilled as usual, but they put this down to her short night.

Pauline was set on having the knife. She counted her money and found she had sixteen shillings. She knew that in Webster's there was even such a knife as she longed for for twelve and nine. She also knew that she was not allowed to have one, for, had she been, they would have given her one for her birthday. She was not allowed to spend birthday money on her own in case she spent it all at once. If she wanted to buy something she had first to ask if she might. She would not be allowed to buy the knife, she knew, nor did she want them to realize quite how badly she wanted it, as it might seem rather ungrateful. But her money was her own after all, so she would get that knife somehow, even though she would not be able to wear it, because then they would see. But to have it, to be able to take it out of her cupboard and feel it, to know it was her own...this would be almost as good as wearing it. She would get it somehow.

She, Nanny and Jelly went shopping that morning. Pauline hated Slater's. As there were always crowds of people waiting to be served there, and Father's jam and bacon had to be so very special, the Children were often allowed to go and look at books in Smith's next door so as not to become too bored and fidgety. That, Pauline realized, was to be her chance.

She was allowed to go to Smith's as usual, while Jelly stayed with Nanny. Instead she dashed over the road, hardly looking where she was going, and was detained for a few moments by a quizzical policeman, to whom she was rather rude. Then she pushed hurriedly on to Webster's, not caring how many people she knocked into, and only just managing to avoid old Mr. Jenkins, the organist. She felt rather shy about asking for the knife, as she realized that it was a strange thing for her to buy. She told them not to wrap it up, because she wanted to be able to feast her eyes on it as she went along, having no time to do so then. She remembered too late that Nanny was not to know about it. She stood and pretended to look into the shop window while actually she surreptitiously undid her coat and fixed the knife on to the belt of her dress. She felt guilty.

She hurried back to Smith's, but was too late, as Nanny emerged from Slater's just before she had time to slip into Smith's.

And then Pauline did a dreadful thing. She committed the unforgivable sin. She told a lie. Nanny wanted to know why she had not been in Smith's, and so Pauline said she had been to Webster's. When Nanny asked why, she said she had been to spend some of her money. It grew worse and worse because Nanny wanted to know what she had bought. In desperation Pauline said she had been to see if there were a doll's tea-set she liked which would do for the new doll, but that there had not been. Nanny grunted disapprovingly about 'not going off like that without asking' but that she 'supposed, as it was her birthday...'

Jelly realized that Pauline was feeling guilty and had done something naughty. He looked curiously at her, but did not say anything.

When they arrived home Pauline took off her coat without thinking, and there was the knife fixed to her belt... There was a dreadful scene...

Pauline was called naughty, disobedient, and a liar. As she knew she was, and yet was not sorry, she did not reply, but just screamed. Nanny screamed too, and Jelly began to cry. Then everyone appeared, and they were told, and the knife was taken away. Pauline had dinner alone in her bedroom. Everything was awful and life was not worth living. There was nothing to do but scream, so she screamed.

She was having a birthday party, and so she could not be left to scream all afternoon. Nanny and Mosey tried to calm her. It was hopeless because she was not sorry and wanted her knife back, and they would not return it and could not forgive her. Father would not go to her. Even The Hump was unable to close his ears and mind to all the noise and misery, and, in any case, he did not want the party to be spoilt. He liked parties. So he went to Pauline, after all the others had been unsuccessful, Gil having been too elder-brotherly and patronizing, and Denise too gently reproving. He did not try to talk to her, but instead read aloud from one of her new books. Because he could not give back the knife, and did not ask her to tell another lie by saying she was sorry, and because the book was interesting, Pauline gradually became quiet. After half an hour or so Nanny was able to wash and dress her for the party.

Strangely enough it was the best party Pauline had ever had. Perhaps she enjoyed it particularly because the preceding anguish enhanced its joy by contrast, but probably it was chiefly because she got her knife after all.

She had been to tea with the Martin's recently, and had amused Mrs. Martin by saying that she wanted a sheath knife with a goat's foot handle more than anything else in the world. Mrs. Martin liked boyish little girls because her's were not and she had no sons. Susie and Pamela were supplied with a knife from Webster's, identical to Pauline's recent acquisition, to present to her when they went to her birthday party. Pauline was thrilled. Mosey saw her open the parcel, but she did not take the knife away, even after the Martin's had been shown upstairs and she could have without seeming rude. And Pauline knew they would not take it away, because that would have been stealing. To be given a knife as a present was quite different from buying it for yourself, even though you bought it with birthday present money.

The party she enjoyed immensely, until just at the very end when she and Ron Cromie began to wrestle and Father came over and coldly told her to behave herself. The other presents were all things she liked, and tea was delicious. The games were fun, and she always loved it when Father showed cinema films, as he did that evening. When it was all over it was bedtime, and Pauline went to sleep with a cosy contented feeling.

Next morning she was spanked.

They did not take away her second sheath-knife because it was a present. They took the one that she had bought back to Webster's and exchanged it for a work-box [sewing case], which Pauline did not want, but which Mosey said she ought to have and would 'appreciate in a year or two'. And she was spanked.

It was after breakfast that it happened. Pauline was taken by surprise because she thought that, as it had been her birthday, she would have been let off. But she was not. When, after breakfast, Mosey came to 'The Nurseries' and said:

'Pauline, your Father wants you in the Study for a few moments dear,' she knew what was going to happen. He was never 'her' Father, nor wanted her for 'a few moments,' nor did Mosey ever call her 'dear' in that tone of voice unless she were going to be spanked.

Pauline dreaded spankings. It was not so much because a spanking hurt, as because she realized what a degrading and undignified punishment it was. Pauline always liked to be considered 'grown-up for her age.' And she hated all the preliminary proceedings that seemed almost to amount to ritual, so carefully were they always carried out. She was spanked quite frequently because she often had scenes with Nanny or Mosey, or squabbled with Jelly, but that did not make any difference. It was always just as bad.

Very occasionally The Hump was beaten too — usually when he had been careless or forgetful about something, but he never seemed to mind much, and it was soon over, while Pauline was sometimes in the Study for as long as twenty minutes, so pitifully did she beg for leniency and so minutely did Father explain why, much as he would like to, he could not spare her. The Hump did not cry or bother any more about it when it was over. This may have been because he never seemed to mind anything much, or possibly it was because he was caned with his trousers on and was not smacked on the bare seat, and because he leaned over the arm of a chair instead of being bent across Father's knees. Pauline realized quite a lot of things, scarcely knowing that she did. She realized that it was the intimacy of a spanking, as much as anything, that made her hate and dread it. Father and The Hump were not on intimate terms and so the caning of The Hump was a cool prosaic operation. When she was spanked it was a protracted and almost lingering ceremony, because she, much more than the others, was intimate with Father.

She knocked on the Study door, and there was Father with his back to the fireplace. He sat down and took her on his knee. Stroking her hair, he said how fond of her he was and how grieved he was at her naughtiness. He was forced to 'deal sharply' with her, he went on, but hated having to do so. Pauline wished he would not cuddle her on his knee like that. It seemed so hypocritical in view of what was to follow. She argued, but he reasoned it all away. She pleaded, begged, implored, but he was firm. She scowled. She hated Father sometimes.

And then he placed her across his knees. Pauline knew that he 'placed' her, and did not merely 'put' her. She knew that he loved her, and she quite loved him too sometimes — as much as she loved anyone — but at the same time she realized that he rather enjoyed spanking her, which made it worse. She was never beaten by anyone else, as Jelly, Hilary and The Hump sometimes were. She knew that he liked it because she was his favourite and he enjoyed to feel his power over her, and because she was plump and squealed.

He folded her frock neatly back, and smoothed it with his hand. Very gently — too gently — he drew down her knickers. That was the worst moment, that moment of infradig exposure. She struggled a little, but he held her firmly in position. Just for a second the palm of his hand rested on her seat, the tips of his fingers slightly kneading the flesh, and then he spanked and it hurt. Pauline squealed.

When it was over, and she was alone in her bedroom, she went on squealing because she always did after she had been spanked. She had been treated like a baby and so it did not matter if she acted like one. Everything was black and hopeless and she wished she were dead. She did not want the old knife any more. It would only make her think of being spanked. She threw it with all her might out of the window and down among the bushes... She bit the curtains... She ripped off her gollywog's legs...

* * *

As children we were beaten not only for genuine bad behaviour but also for such things as breaking windows by mistake and carelessly leaving doors open. Keith was, for a time, beaten every Thursday for biting his nails. When we strip-washed together one morning I was astounded to see purple wheals on his buttocks. My spankings and canings never resulted in more than a ruddy glow or a few pink stripes. As I grew older I felt increasingly both humiliated and, in a sense, violated, by the paternal beatings I continued to receive on my bare buttocks. After Nanny left when I was nine (a traumatic experience for me) I received as much (if not more) corporal punishment as before, as my parents, now fully in charge of me for the first time, discovered that I was a much more tiresome child than they had previously supposed. By the time I was ten my mother decided that this form of punishment was no longer suitable for a daughter, and my father reluctantly agreed that it should end.

5

Christmases, like birthdays and summer holidays, were the high spots in my otherwise rather dull life — which consisted mainly of lessons, going shopping with Nanny, then, after tea and listening to 'Children's Hour' on the wireless, embroidering tray-cloths for church sales of work (bazaars) while Nanny read me Arthur Ransom and Angela Brazil stories until bedtime at half past six. We indicated what presents we wanted (I burned my letter to Father Christmas in traditional fashion up the chimney — but not until I had first let the grown-ups see it...). There was bitter frustration one year when the long-awaited Christmas Day had to be postponed until Boxing Day as December 25th fell on a Sunday and my parents (partly, no doubt, to stave off the potential wrath of my ultra-pious grandmother) decided it would be 'breaking the Sabbath' to do anything so secular as celebrate Christmas on a Sunday.

Our Christmas parties were usually enlivened by my father showing Charlie Chaplin films and home movies or giving a conjuring show (as well as being a parson he was a life-long, quite well-known and sought-after amateur magician who both performed and invented tricks).

Presumably Christmas was more fun for us children than

for our mother who, although a very good vicar's wife who spoke well at meetings and helped organise parish events, was, nevertheless, apt to get flustered, worked up and peevish. She often 'made mountains out of molehills' — increasingly so after World War II broke out and all our domestics soon vanished, including Nanny, on whom she had greatly relied. Mosey in *Multicolour* is not unlike her, and her story is in a way the story of our family Christmases. For although my mother revelled in Christmas, carols, Christmas trees and all things Christmasy (and I caught or inherited this passion from her), the preparations and actual day, once she was a vicar's wife and mother, must have been in many ways tiring and trying.

'Mosey' (a chapter from *Multicolour*)

Mosey found most things difficult. She had not always done so. When she was a girl, life had been uneventful and very simple — perhaps too simple, for, when she suddenly found herself a housewife, vicar's wife, and mother of a family, difficulties doubled themselves by contrast, and mole-hills reared up into formidable mountain ranges.

Fortunately, there was Nanny, who was three of the four legs that supported the family table. She was indispensable. But despite Nanny life was fraught with difficulty, for, after all, Mosey did not realise that Nanny made all the important decisions, while she merely fell in with them. She thought that she herself was the family arbitress. Nor was Henry very much use. He was a final court of appeal, but, as he considered matters ecclesiastical and fiscal to be his sole province, he resigned all else to Mosey, saying:

'Well my dear, that's up to you to decide.' And so Nanny had to exercise her wits again.

Mosey hated Christmas. Had she allotted separate colours to the seasons, Christmas would not have been pillar-box red, as it was for Hilary. It was fraught with more difficulty than any other time throughout the year.

Christmas Day itself was but the climax of protracted difficulties extending over a period of weeks.

There were the parties. They were hectic enough when they actually happened, but the preliminary arrangements were almost worse. There were all the games that had to be thought out. This was not easy because there had to be different sorts of games and entertainments for each different party. The Junior Sunday School could be made to play 'oranges and lemons' and 'musical bumps' happily all afternoon. The Seniors were quite content to play 'general post' for some time, provided there were a good tea and a Punch and Judy Show afterwards. But the Choir, what for them? The ages of its members varied between seven and seventy. The small boys gobbled so rapidly and, as there could not be inexhaustible plates of food, the time for 'refreshments' could not be protracted indefinitely. The Choir men could not be forced to play 'murder' or 'sardines', and the boys could not be coerced into playing pencil and paper games, which were 'just like school.' It was alright if they arrived late, so that eating could start promptly, as immediately afterwards, Mr. Blenkinsop could give his annual film show, after which the party ended. But they usually arrived early rather than late, and stampeded for an hour or so. It bothered Mosey to feel people were stampeding. Mr. Blenkinsop's repertoire was now exhausted, and occasionally such whispers as: 'Blimey — daft old Charlie slinging custard round again! Seen it twice already' would be heard.

The Women's party was worse. The Women were too physically decrepit for musical bumps, and too mentally decrepit for pencil and paper games. They criticised the food. Old Mrs. Hopcraft regularly said: 'Had meringues up at Baptist's a week ago, I did, and cream jelly down at Congregational.' This was disconcerting, as Mosey never supplied The Women with such expensive luxuries.

The entertainment part of the proceedings was difficult too. The Women were old both in years and membership of the Meeting, and so there could be no question as to whether, in their case, Mr. Blenkinsop's stock of cinema-films had been exhausted. Once Mosey had tried Punch and Judy on them and Mrs. Hopcraft had been heard to mumble: 'That's summer, that is. Can see that down on beach any day in summer.' Sometimes Mr. Jacobs gave a reading and recitation in dialect. The Women would cackle, but, as they themselves all spoke in broad dialect, either the point of the entertainment must have been entirely lost on them, or else if sufficiently intelligent, they must have been slightly offended. Mrs. Hopcraft had once muttered, loudly: 'Don't see anything funny in that, I don't,' until nudged and hushed by her next door neighbour. To prevent them all spending the afternoon just clustering and gossiping Mosey had to strain the neighbourhood in the hope of extracting a conjuror. Anybody could understand and appreciate the production of coloured streamers from obviously empty brass tubes.

Most of the parish parties were 'got over' before Christmas, but the Church Party and the Children's party were both held very soon after Christmas, and so all preparations had to be made before.

Problems arose over the Church Party as it was open to any 'regular member of the congregation' provided he arrived with food to contribute to the pooled refreshments. But who was a 'regular member of the congregation'? — what precise qualities did this imply? There were some who seemed to be 'regular members' because they appeared at all the more secular parochial functions, and quite often lent a hand at organizing them. Nevertheless they did not darken the Church doors more than four or five times in the year because either it was 'too wet to go out' or else 'too fine not to go for a picnic.' To such, it ought by right to be intimated that they were not eligible for the Church Party.

As it was impossible to ascertain how many would turn up (one year twenty appeared, and the next sixty-four) it was hard to know what sort of games to arrange. The Church Party was rather an important function as it was supposed annually to typify the good fellowship of the 'regular members of the congregation,' and thereby to stimulate good fellow-ship and regular membership. The party had therefore to be very enjoyable and well organized. There had to be those carefully planned games which entail much printing on cards, cutting up of paper slips, and pinning of notices on to walls.

There were difficulties about refreshments too. Who would be willing to help spread tables, hand round, wash up?

The final problem arose because of Henry's insistence that a religious element should be introduced into the proceed-ings. Mosey never dared gainsay him in this. She herself approved of opening and closing prayers, but could not help noticing that hymn-singing was not performed with much gusto. There was no getting away from it, the members of the congregation, however regular, did not want religion wedged into their Christmas party. A brief survey of the work of the C.M.S. in South India, interjected between 'mixed groceries' and 'duster hockey', seemed out of place, while a 'missionary brains' trust', as Mosey knew at the back of her mind, was but a hypocritical way of giving a series of camouflaged mission-ary talks. What form should the religious element take?...

Although Henry considered parochial affairs his sphere, yet church parties were essentially domestic affairs. So closely connected were they with laying tables and making sand-wiches, that he left them to Mosey to deal with. To Mosey, not realizing how much of the organisation fell into Nanny's hands, they all seemed very very difficult.

Nor was the Children's Party a simple matter, because everyone seemed to want something different. Jelly insisted on éclairs while Pauline was equally firm that it should be meringues. It was impossible to manage both.

There was not room for more than a limited number of boisterous juvenile guests in the china-incrusted drawing-room. The Children invariably had different long lists of friends to invite, and squabbled among themselves if one of them seemed to be having more than his or her fair share. Pauline always wanted to ask Mickey, who had red hair. Mickey was the most obstreporous child in the neighbourhood, and he fought more violently and stampeded more bewilderingly than any other boy in the town. One year he had filled up all the other children's outdoor shoes with water when he was supposed to be playing 'musical parcel'. After he had smashed the glass door of a cabinet and thrown a small china vase across the drawingroom at Pauline's head, Father issued an edict that he was to be invited to no more parties. Mickey's mother never gave parties and so they were under no obligation to him. But Mickey was 'so exciting' that Pauline always wanted to invite him...

The Children all wanted different sorts of games and entertainments. The Hump favoured a film show, while Pauline and Jelly were all for a conjuror. Hilary obviously hated 'blind man's buff' and preferred charades, which made Pauline call her 'stupid and dull.'

Even The Angel was a problem. She was too old for the Children's party, but not considered old enough for the Grown-up's coffee parties. Whenever parties were under discussion she assumed an injured 'left-out' expression.

This Christmas was more difficult than any previous one had been — at least so it seemd to Mosey, but then she felt like this about every Christmas in turn. The parties were all quite as difficult to arrange as ever — on the whole, more so. Somehow or another Mickey was coming to the Children's party after all. Mrs. Hopcraft had, as usual, remarked on the cream jelly she had eaten 'up Baptists''. The conjuror had been wrung out of the neighbourhood only after extreme exertion and endless enquiries. Mr. Blenkinsop had, by mistake, given a film show identical to last year's...

Food. The subject of Christmas food had always to be considered months in advance. Mosey began to hoard up dried fruit for the cake and pudding right back in August while the family was still away on the summer holiday. [This reflects our World War II situation.]

An almond-icing tragedy occurred. For some obscure reason it was found by Hilary, whose turn it was to scrape out the sugar basin, that the almond-icing tasted 'kind of soapy'.

It did. Mosey swore her to secrecy in the matter, hoping doubtfully either that Henry's acute palate might not detect the soapyness, or that she might in some way — perhaps by adding a good deal more almond essence with just a suspicion of vanilla — manage to camouflage the unfortunate flavour.

The Christmas pudding seemed a trifle too moist when turned out, and Gil always stressed the importance of having a 'good square pudding' which he could 'get his teeth into'. There were other difficulties about the pudding. Brass three-penny-bits were supposed to be poisonous, but Mosey had no silver ones to put in it. Henry, when consulted, said that 'The Children were never satisfied' and that the pudding ought to be 'quite good enough as it was'. Mosey knew quite well that it would not be. Then Jelly slyly removed all the shilling and half-crown pieces from her purse and plunged them into the pudding mixture. She found out. Jelly was scolded, and cried because he said he had only been 'trying to help'. Nanny said grimly: 'Trying to help himself, that's what,' which made Jelly cry all the more. Finally Mosey compromised by letting him stir in a few sixpences instead.

An ugly turkey question arose as ever to darken the foreground of Christmas week...

Presents seemed to be more of a problem than ever. The Children all wanted such impossible things. Jelly pined for a green parrot that could talk. Henry had once said: 'No pets,' and had only, with difficulty, been cajoled into tolerating the presence of the innocuous Growler. A green parrot, especially if loquacious, was therefore impossible as a present. Jelly would have to be content with a toy, squeaking one, and Mosey knew he would not be... The Hump wanted a gramophone, but gramophones were 'such a price,' besides, they were no use without records as well... The Angel was difficult because she did not ask for anything in particular, and so was likely to be displeased with whatever she was given. There was nothing, of course, that Gil wanted which was not either extremely expensive or else unobtainable. The only people for whom it was comparatively easy to buy presents were

Denise and Henry. Denise was always pleased with anything, or, at any rate, appeared to be. Henry she regularly presented with a book token and a new blotter.

Christmas Day began for Mosey as soon as Christmas Eve ended. This was because of Jelly. The Hump and Hilary were too old to believe any longer in Father Christmas. Pauline wavered a little and still believed when it seemed profitable to do so. But Jelly was still beneath the spell of Fairyland, which no one, not even Pauline, who enjoyed Nanny's fairy tales told for his benefit, had attempted to break. He had not yet begun to wonder how Father Christmas fitted into the chimney, nor how, within a few hours, he could visit the homes of all the children in the world. And so at midnight there had to be a Father Christmas for Jelly to see. He was woken, very carefully so that he should not know that someone had woken him. Henry was cajoled into deferring going to bed, and was pinned into a stretch of frayed red material, erratically fringed with white wisps. Jelly's stocking was filled under his eyes, and, afterwards, he had to be persuaded not to open it till morning. He would fall asleep again only by being told a story...

There was early awakening for Mosey too. Sudden pandemonium burst into the bedroom, her warm comfortable sleep was exploded, and she was plunged violently into Christmas Day. A horde of stocking-bearing children swarmed over the bed. Soon bits of paper and orange peel were scattered everywhere, semi-sucked fruit-drops were congealing on the sheets, tin whistles shrilled, and 'stocking-presents' were being flaunted, envied, quarrelled over and swapped...Pauline was there to be played with, and so Henry did not mind. When she was properly awake Mosey did not mind either. She forgot to regret the rough intrusion on her sleep and entered into The Children's spirit.

When she was up difficulties started to crowd at her, and her festive spirit evaporated. After breakfast The Children began to clamour and be tiresome, and Nanny summoned her to try to exercise authority. Pauline had lost interest in her 'stocking-presents' and wanted to have her bigger ones, which were reserved until after dinner, now. She could not be scolded as it was Christmas Day. She had to be soothed without being given in to...a very difficult business.

Suddenly The Hump said firmly that he wanted to read his new book all morning, and would not go to Church. He was very seldom firmly defiant like this, but, when he was, it was well nigh impossible to move him. No arguments or persuasions moved him this time. A deadlock was reached until it suddenly dawned upon him that he was spoiling Christmas for Mosey, and he remembered that there would be a long time between dinner and 'presents' to be filled in somehow.

It crossed Mosey's mind to wonder why she herself went to Church on Christmas Day. There were all the extensive dinner preparations to be made, and yet nobody seemed to be in a hurry to get home after Church and 'get on'. Old Mr. Blenkinsop kept them shivering in the churchyard for a solid five minutes while he talked about his brother-in-law in California. Miss Jacks stopped to wish them a Merry Christmas, and went on to explain at great length how she always got her 'thank you letters' written before Christmas. Mosey did not, and did not want to hear about it. Mrs. Jenkins gushed protractedly at them outside the garden gate about Christmas being a 'jolly time for the Little Ones.'

At last they were back. Christmas dinner was at midday and she and Nanny 'got down to it.' This was the worst part of the day. In spite of Nanny and Mable things seemed to get beyond her. She tried to polish the special table silver, chivy off the interloping Children, and beat up the cream all at the same moment. Where had those tinned-strawberries got to? Why was the cut-glass sugar-bowl cracked? — it had not been before. the mince-pies! — suddenly she remembered that she had forgotten to bake them after all yesterday... Orange-squash for the table? The egg-whisk? Cherries? Why had the jellies not set properly?... Mable, where had she got to?... Burning!...

She was unable even to enjoy the meal properly. She had to

keep hurrying off to the larder and kitchen for little things that had been over-looked. Nanny and The Children came into the dining room for Christmas dinner, and the latter began to grow 'a little over-excited'. They kept blowing their shrill cracker whistles... Henry began to look a trifle resigned... The Children had to be hushed, but they would not be...

'Lois, I wish you would do a little bread-sauce another time. You know how fond of it I am dear.' Could she really have forgotten about the bread-sauce again? So many things, which she alone could find, seemed to have been left outside, that she could not sit still and enjoy her meal. She just started to get down to it, as it was beginning to cool off and congeal, when the others passed up their plates for second helpings, and she had to leave off eating again.

After the meal Henry said: 'Children to their quarters now.'

Nanny drove them off, and the Grown-ups retired to doze down their meal in the warm drawing room for an hour or so. But Mosey could not relax. She kept hearing sounds of distant petulance. At last she could bear it no longer. Gil muttered, 'Where the Hell are you hopping off to now Mosey?' Henry raised one drowsily disapproving eyelid.

She found that Hilary had been sick, and that Nanny was scolding Jelly for taking iced dates away from the table in his pockets. Pauline was running up and down and loudly wanting her presents. Mosey tried unsuccessfully to calm them all down, considerably adding to the uproar in her attempts. She returned to Henry. After much coaxing, interrupted by disgruntled growls from Gil, she managed to persuade Henry to bestir himself and allow 'presents' to begin. She lit the Christmas-Tree candles and drew the curtains in order to create a mysterious festive atmosphere. The Children, Nanny, and Mable were summoned. The distribution began.

Mosey was not able to enjoy even this. The Christmas Tree candles kept dripping grease on to the carpet. It was a struggle against overwhelming odds for her and Nanny to attempt to keep a list of all The Children's presents, so that they should not forget to whom they had to write 'thank you letters.' Suddenly a sprig of Christmas Tree caught fire. Nanny and Gil simultaneously plunged masterfully forward to quench the flames... Jelly's new toy watch was trodden on and dented. He began to cry... So did The Chit...

When she had time to think about it, Mosey felt anxious about The Children's reception of their presents. Luckily Jelly had realized that a talking parrot was too much to hope for, and so was fairly satisfied with his toy one. The Hump's disappointment, as Mosey happened to notice, at the non-appearance of a gramophone was quite apparent for a few seconds after he had unwrapped the book that was given to him instead. The Angel's customary blaséness over most of her presents was obvious as usual, and Pauline, who got what she wanted, was almost too excited about it... As for her own presents, there just did not seem to be time to unwrap many of them, and they remained done up until next day.

Tea, with Christmas Cake, which should have been delicious, was not fully appreciated as everyone had eaten too much dinner. Mosey felt bothered the whole time because there was so much paper, string and 'riff-raff' about the room. She longed to clear it up straight away, but knew she must leave it scattered exasperatingly around until later when she could gather it up at her leisure without being collided into by hurtling Children.

The period between tea and bedtime was dreadful. Christmas Day was really over and The Children began to wonder what to do next and to squabble over swapping their presents. Henry refused to forfeit a peaceful evening's reading in order to join in round-the-table games. Denise suddenly felt tired and went off to bed. Gil decided to 'go over the way and see how Old Jack was getting on', which seemed all wrong on Christmas Night. The Angel kept clamouring for somebody to play ping-pong with her. In the background Nanny kept chivying The Children, who screamed and stampeded until finally sent off to bed. Mable went 'off' without leave, and so

Nanny and Mosey had to prepare supper. When it was ready Henry did not seem to have any appetite, Gil was still out, and Denise was in bed, so that Mosey found there was only herself and the somewhat morose and dispirited Angel to eat it. All of a sudden Mosey wanted to go to bed too...

As she was dropping off to sleep she realized in a cosily contented way that The Awful Day was over for another year, and that it would be impossible to go shopping tomorrow anyway...

Daddy (oil; age fifteen)

Torquay: View from my Home (oil; age fourteen)

6

My father believed in changing parishes periodically. We moved from Leamington Spa to Weston-super-Mare when I was four. I was very excited when told we were going to live at the seaside — even though warned that there would be more mud than sea at Weston. The first night in the new vicarage I stood at my parents' bedroom window staring fascinated at the distant strings of lights along the Promenade and pier. I have always loved glass and lights. I was nine when, just before the war broke out, we moved from Weston to Torquay and even better seaside. Again I was delighted when I learned we were moving.

My first 'school' was not really a school: it was a collection of eight or nine upper-class Torquay children of varying ages (including two little boys) who were taught by the governess of one of them, there being no 'suitable' schools in the town. I called this gathering 'The Class'. As I was the oldest member of it (I was nine and Nanny had just left), even though I was a new pupil I became, in effect, head girl immediately and quite enjoyed the unearned distinction. But this fairly happy state of affairs lasted less than a year. By the time I was ten a 'suitable' school had arrived in Torquay: Farringtons, a Methodist girls' boarding school evacuated from Kent. It was housed in a Babbacombe hotel, a couple of the classrooms (including mine) being screened-off portions of the large dining-room and the 'lab' an erstwhile guests' bedroom. The school survived in its new premises for only about a year then went into liquidation until the end of the war.

I did not at all enjoy my first couple of terms. There were very few daygirls, and the boarders remained aloof and contemptuous of us. It was the Westcliff dancing class all over again. I was exceedingly shy and nervous. This was partly because I was a daygirl and partly because I was almost the youngest in the class. It was also partly because of Nanny's endless evening reading to me of girls' school stories, which, coupled with the fact that I went to school relatively late, gave me an inflated idea of what school was — or should be. They made it seem more awe-inspiring, awful and important than might have been the case had I first gone when I was six or seven, as my contemporaries did. Had I done so, I might have been better able to 'take school in my stride'.

To start with, I was in the bottom class, where the age range was eight to twelve. Although practically the youngest in the class, I came second in exams. It was all very confusing. And I fell seriously in love for the first time — with Daphne, the popular, twelve-year-old Form Captain. This was long before I knew about sex, but, looking back, it seems to me that my hero-worship of Daphne was tinged with eroticism. I still have her ruler, inscribed with her name, which somehow came into my possession — I am using it at this very moment.

I was so timid that I was 'as good as gold' (at school if not at home) for my first couple of terms at Farringtons. One day one of the older girls in my class said 'Do *try* to be naughty, Pat.' It was a moment of truth and a turning point in my life. I then realised that, to be at all popular, or even tolerated, I had to stop being good. I was in a quandary: what about Christianity and the wickedness of 'sinning'? That evening I deeply shocked my devout old grandmother — by then living with and trying to tyrannize over us — by saying 'Gran, I do wish I could be naughty.' She was incredulous — however naughty children might be, surely they did not actually *want* to be, and anyway, as far as she was concerned, I was naughty. Ironically, good though I was, at school, at that time my school report stated that I 'did not think enough about others' (which was no doubt in a sense true as I was so shy). Miss Bradley, the headmistress, took me to task over this and pointed out that it was not a 'very Guidey' report (she was an ardent adult Girl Guide).

So I set about trying to be naughty. It was difficult at first, then became all too easy. I forced myself to be cheeky to the teachers; I was kept behind after school to do extra work as a punishment... Yet my next report said I was 'now thinking much more of others.'

'That's much more Guidey, Pat,' Miss Bradley said kindly. I was baffled. However, I was never really good again. Later, at Stover, I was once even told I was 'past punishing'. I was delighted and have often wished the various magistrates and judges who have passed sentence on me since had reached the same conclusion.

During the last term of the school's existence there was an influx of daygirls. I was no longer new and almost the youngest in the school. I moved into a higher form, managed to get naughtier and naughtier, acquired a Best Friend and a number of more casual ones and became quite happy.

After Farringtons disbanded I went to Stover (a small, private girls' school where I was a boarder from the age of ten to fourteen), some twelve miles away in the country. (To the displeasure of Miss Dence, the headmistress, I used — unlike the other girls — to bicycle to and fro at the beginning and end of term. My parents didn't mind: it saved money. They were a very economical couple; quite stingy, in fact — my diary includes lamentations over the paucity of my pocket money.) The school was a converted former duke's 'country seat' set in a large park, which we were not allowed to wander about in unaccompanied — presumably because of all the troops in the vicinity. I was ten when I went there. My parents by then felt they couldn't cope with me so handed me over to others who might manage better. In a sense I was 'put in care' because I was 'beyond control' — anyway as far as they were concerned.

For the first term or two it was Westcliff and Farringtons all over again. I was thoroughly disliked. To this day I don't really know why — presumably I was nasty. Anyway, I was miserable, homesick (even though not very happy at home either) and did badly at everything. I was the youngest in the form and put in a dormitory with girls my own age and younger who were academically my juniors, which made my position ambiguous and was not conducive to making friends. As before, the situation improved after a couple of terms. I decided to assume the role of clown and gradually settled down and made some friends. I ceased to be inept at games and began to do quite well at work.

However, although I was no longer unpopular with my fellow-pupils I became exceedingly unpopular with my school-mistresses. Having gone through an initial period of relative shyness, as at Farringtons I again found it paid, as regards my relations with my contemporaries, to be naughty; so I was. I was caught one night in a dormitory pillow fight by the ferocious, prison-officer-like Matron (later sacked for anti-Semitism and telling us our parents would all fall ill and die if we misbehaved). She told me I was a 'black, evil girl' and 'a hypocrite' because my father was a parson (even at the time I could see this was a non-sequitur). She asked if I had ever seen my face in a mirror — to which I gave our stock, safe response to such questions from members of the school staff.

'I don't know, Matron,' I lied.

Two consecutive chapters in *Those Happiest Days* (my first novel written when I was fifteen to sixteen) about two totally fictitious and fairly improbable incidents show how I felt as a New Girl at all my schools — except The Class.

'An Episode Connected with a Lavatory'
(a chapter from *Those Happiest Days*)

That first term was rather a miserable one for Pip. Oddly enough, Miss Parker wrote on her end-of-term report: 'A good term. Philippa seems to have settled down quite satisfactorily.' It was the best conduct report that Pip ever had. From that time on each succeeding report seemed a shade worse than the one before.

As a matter of fact it was neither a 'good term', nor did Pip 'settle down' at all 'satisfactorily'. This was chiefly owing to the shyness, self-consciousness and general feeling of newness that clung to her throughout the term, which, often scarcely knowing they did, or why they did, her school-fellows exploited. Nobody who has not suffered the ignominy of invariably being chosen last to help make up a side in a game can quite understand the wretched unwanted feeling that most new girls have during their first few weeks at school...

She suffered because people said: 'Oh, that kid would,' when she passed to someone on the opposite side by mistake in a game of lacrosse; because people sometimes giggled, whispered, and pointed at her for quite obscure reasons; because people said: 'Oh, get out, can't you', when she came over to their desks to see photos that they were showing to the others; because often they would say 'What a beastly skirt, all dirty and shapeless', when it was a skirt that she was rather proud of; because all the people she liked or admired ignored her, and because wherever she was, and whoever she was with, she always felt unwanted and in the way.

Pip spent some of the most agonising moments of her life on Sunday mornings. On Sundays you were allowed to sit anywhere at the meal table instead of in allotted places, as on week-days. Pip could not think why, but there was always one place short. By the time she reached the dining-room all the places were always 'bagged' — although often she noticed that as soon as she had moved away they promptly became 'unbagged' again. She would drift helplessly around the room in search of somewhere to sit, and finally would ask whether she might go to the kitchen and fetch herself the necessary articles for eating. She would then have to try to fit in at the end of a table next to a mistress, while all the others on the bench muttered curses quite audibly, and those on the other side of the table gazed across at her in scorn.

Going to church was worse than anything. Although, summoning all her courage, Pip would ask all sorts of people to be her partner, she always knew that they would refuse, and that she would be obliged to sink to the ignominy of walking with Anne Markby, a small, despised, new girl, four years her junior, and Helen Smith, the heavy pig-tailed new girl, with whom she had shared a taxi at the beginning of term, and who had become the butt of the school.

One Sunday, towards the end of term, she could bear it no more. She had spilt ink on the form-room floor when writing her letter home. Bob [short for Roberta] was Form Captain, and, advancing brandishing a ruler threateningly, had said: 'You ruddy little fool. You damn well go down and get something to clear up the muck with.' Pip went down, fetched a cloth, wiped the mess up, and then finished her letter without saying anything. As a rule, when people teased her or shouted at her, she just felt like crying from the sheer misery and loneliness of life, but this time, although she felt like crying and could hardly restrain herself from doing so, she also felt thoroughly roused by Bob's hectoring tones. After all, at home they weren't always 'going on' at her, and at home she wasn't bad at everything... She could beat Dick Frobisher at swimming, and once had even beaten Uncle Claud at table-tennis when he was playing left-handed. Why should Bob think that she was bad at everything? She'd jolly well show them all... She jolly well wouldn't ask any of them to be her church partner, they could just do without her. What was more, she wouldn't go with silly old fat Helen Smith, nor with that kid Anne Markby. With whom should she go then? What should she do?... She jolly well wouldn't go at all — not if she knew it. This was the essence of Pip's thoughts as she sat writing her home letter.

At about ten-thirty a bell rang, and immediately the whole school was in an uproar. Desks slammed, doors banged, shouts resounded from room to room, and bodies charged at a quite unlawful speed down passages, colliding violently with each other from time to time...

The noise and turmoil which accompanied the bell for church that Sunday was useful from Pip's point of view. Everyone was too busy to notice when, armed with 'The Murderer in Black,' she retired inconspicuously to one of the lavatories, to spend a more enthralling, if somewhat less spiritually elevating, morning than she would have seated crushed between Helen Smith and Anne Markby on a hard church pew, counting the number of words begining with 'c' that the vicar used in his sermon.

Pip saw no reason why anybody should find out how she spent the morning. There was only a small chance that her absence from church would be noticed, and, locked away in a lavatory, nobody would be able to discover her in the building. She forgot that Matron was not a zealous church attendant...

Although 'Oaklands' was an old manor house, which at one time had been the country seat of Lord so-and-so, Miss Parker's predecessor, the foundress of the school, had had installed every modern convenience, such as electric lighting and a food lift from the kitchen to the dining room. The new lavatories that were created were quite dazzlingly modern, and even had the sort of bolts which, when drawn across, enabled a would-be entrant to see that the place was 'engaged'. In passing, Matron happened to notice that the lavatory was 'engaged', and was mildly surprised, as she had thought that, apart from the servants in the kitchen, she was the only other person in the building. She went on to her room, and then, some little time later, happened to pass by the lavatory once again. It was still apparently 'engaged'. She tried the door. Pip had just arrived at the critical moment in the history of 'The Murderer in Black' — the fearless detective was just about to catch him red-handed trying to strangle a rich young heiress in bed. Suddenly she heard someone try the handle, and went rigid with a terror far greater than that aroused by the most gruesome of assassinations by murderers clad in any colour imaginable.

Finding the door locked, and being of a suspicious nature, Matron decided to sit on a nearby chair and await the exit of the lavatory occupier. The chair was quite comfortable, and Matron, having both an interesting book and a malicious character, was quite content to sit reading, with the pleasant feeling at the back of her mind that some miserable girl was trapped within the lavatory waiting for her departure.

Time passed. Finally the girls returned from church and came upstairs. As each girl passed, Matron explained why she was sitting there, so that soon practically the whole school was gathered around awaiting the appearance of the mysterious occupant of the lavatory, whose identity they had not deduced, as Pip's presence or absence was not a thing which anybody noticed much.

Pip never again in her life, not even during moments of most agonising suspense, spent a more unpleasant quarter of an hour. She heard all that was said, and she knew she must go out and face them all sooner or later. Suddenly Providence sent her an idea. The window. She climbed stealthily on to the seat, looked out, and saw the sloping tiled roof. She could not quite tell what happened at the edge, but it could not be too terribly high above the ground. Anyhow, better anything than to go out and face all those people, and to be laughed at by them all — especially by Ann Jenkins, that tall, pretty prefect, who was clever and good at everything... If she got killed, broke her leg or something, they might all be sorry they had been so beastly... She would be able to leave if she did not actually get killed... Matron might even be sent to prison...

She opened the window noiselessly (it was a casement), climbed on to the window-sill and wormed herself silently out on to the tiles. Cautiously she worked her way down the roof and stood upright on a fairly broad gutter running along the edge. She looked down, and then promptly leaned back against the roof through dizziness. She was three times the height of the top diving-board at home above the ground, but if she managed to jump far enough she would land on the top of the macracarpa hedge, and could climb down from it to the ground...

She gazed at the hedge... Could she? What if she did not? Did getting killed hurt awfully? If she were to die would she go to Heaven? (viewing her past life Pip could not think of any especial reasons in favour of the latter). Anyway, she wasn't going back to that lavatory, and she wasn't going to be laughed at and teased for ever by those beastly girls — better anything...yes definitely anything...

Pip would have broken all records on Sports Day had she jumped as far in the Long Jump as she did that Sunday morning. She landed on the hedge, and fell through it almost to the ground. She crept out from beneath it and lay panting on the grass. She had made a great hole in the hedge, had broken innumerable branches, and was covered with scratches and bruises. After a few minutes, feeling very shaken, she got up and went into the cloakroom, where she washed and tidied herself up. Then she went upstairs, and, unnoticed, joined the crowd outside the lavatory.

Suddenly she wanted to laugh. She could scarcely control herself from bursting into peals of ringing mirth. It was the first time since she had been at 'Oaklands' that she really had felt like laughing. There was Matron, puce with wrath, hammering with all her might and main on the door, and screaming: 'Come out! Come out, will you! This has gone on long enough. Come out! Do you dare defy me? Open the door this instant or I go straight down to Miss Parker.' Then everybody seemed to start shrieking and rushing around. Remarks were hurled indiscriminately right and left. Miss Parker, all the staff, including the Under Matron, Cook and Odd-Jobs, appeared, and further abuse was hurled at the empty lavatory. Finally the door was broken down... The tumult and the shouting gradually died down, the mistresses and girls departed; but Pip had made history. From that time forth the lavatory was regarded as haunted, and girls who had not arrived at years of valour or disillusionment never frequented it after nine at night in summer and five-thirty in winter.

That evening Matron noticed the cuts on Pip's legs. The only comment she made when Pip said she had fallen down in the garden was: 'The other girls don't go doing things like that. You had better let me put something on it for you, and you can go to bed an hour early.'

'April Fool's Day'
(a chapter from *Those Happiest Days*)

The second term was different. Quite why this was so Pip never discovered, but as soon as she arrived back at the beginning of term she noticed the difference. She was in the same dormitory, but her particular enemies, Bob and Mary Hodge — the fluffy-haired girl who had also been new the preceding term, and whom she had disliked at sight — had both moved elsewhere.

The first difference that Pip noticed was the attitude of the rest of the dormitory. No longer did it contain the sort of girls who threw your books and teddy-bears around, whispered and sniggered about you, or openly pulled faces at you. The ring-leaders who had stirred up mockery and teasing for her among the others having left the dormitory, Pip found that the meeker spirits remaining behind were quite willing to let her enter into conversation with them, and, discovering for the first time that she was 'not too bad after all', even started up conversations with her themselves. This attitude of toleration, and even of friendliness, spread further afield than the dormitory, so that, after a week or two, even Bob and 'her lot' were even prepared to laugh at her jokes.

Another thing that seemed to make the beginning of that term quite different from the last was the arrival of Kitty Smale. Looking back in after years Pip sometimes wondered why this had been so. Kitty was smallish and thinnish, with a freckled, ordinary face, a complete absence of eyebrows, and nondescript hair bound back into two absurd tufts which stuck out behind. Pip did not even like her particularly.

It was not so much Kitty's actual presence in the school that made the difference as the fact that Pip was commissioned to 'look after' her. 'Looking after' entailed the performance of all those functions over which Bob had been so negligent on Pip's behalf the previous term. To old-timers in a secure and firmly established position at 'Oaklands' 'looking after' new girls was a 'perfect curse' or a 'confounded nuisance', as it meant 'bagging' them places at table, showing them round, and suffering their society as partners to church instead of walking with their especial friends. To Pip it was the height of bliss to feel responsible about something, to know that there was somebody for whom she could 'bag places' who would do the same for her, and to be able loftily to refuse the companionship of Anne Markby and Helen Smith as partners to church.

It may as well be remarked, before dismissing the subject of Kitty Smale finally, that by half-term Pip had become so much one of the crowd that she lost all self-consciousness and became aware of the desirability of other members of her form as friends in preference to Kitty. This was not surprising as Kitty was all the things that Pip was forever trying not to be, and which in her heart of hearts she despised. She was bad at painting, was completely bored by any music, and enjoyed such obnoxious occupations as knitting jumpers, baking cakes, and working out geometrical problems. Above all she was completely hopeless at games and gym — possibly even worse than herself Pip fondly hoped. Kitty did not especially like Pip, who was always wanting to go off and 'do things', and grumbling because she could not. She found Pip useful as a 'place-bagger' and church partner, but was not genuinely moved when, by half-term, Pip was generally with other rowdier members of the form, leaving her to the more placid companionship of Helen Smith.

These differences, caused by a sense of security, declining unpopularity, and finally growing popularity, caused other even greater differences to come about. Pip no longer felt afraid of mockery if she failed to clear the horse in a vault during a gym lesson, consequently she usually managed to sail over with comparative ease, if not with very graceful style. Then, greatest of joys, there was the Junior Netball Team. To be eligible for a place in a junior team at 'Oaklands' you had to be eleven or under, and most of those who were good at games in Pip's form were twelve or thirteen. The result was that, after one or two trial games, Pip saw her name inscribed on the list of the Junior Second Team as 'centre defence'. The fact that they lost the match did not really matter to her at all. When watching school matches she shouted and clapped with the rest, but often found the intense loyalty and school patriotism, that her strident tones suggested she possessed, rather difficult to muster. She was young enough and new enough to her school not to mind much when they lost the match by four goals, but, like most people, she was sufficiently self-centred to be over-joyed by such remarks made to her afterwards as: 'Gosh, Pip, you're jolly good — I always thought you were rotten at games'.

There was a marked difference between the conduct reports of Pip's first and second terms. The Very Reverend Humphrey Sladen read with a perturbed spirit at the end of Pip's second term that although she had 'evidently settled down quite happily', yet she seemed sadly lacking in that indispensible of qualities at a girls' school, namely 'discipline'. ['Discipline', or lack of same, was a term constantly flung at me throughout my childhood, especially my schooldays.] For by her second term at 'Oaklands' Pip had learnt one of the great truths connected with schoolgirls at the age of approximately eleven to fourteen. To be popular you must on no account whatever be 'good': and so, to avoid the horror of being so described, she indulged in an orgy of nocturnal pillow-fights, repartee with mistresses, and water-bomb throwing during lesson times.

April Fool's Day was the last Monday of term, and the events of that day finally brought about Miss Parker's decision to give Pip only a very mediocre conduct report. Of course all the usual things happened. The post was enlarged by the presence of many letters whose brief contents could be summed up in two words. Amid general mirth it was found that both the teapots at breakfast were empty, and that the legs of the chairs at the Staff Table were tied together...

But all of this was mere child's play, just what was expected, what had been done from time immemorial, and what would continue to be done until the final dissolution of 'Oaklands'. Pip fully realised this. She also knew that if she surpassed tradition and performed a really spectacular 'April Fool', her growing popularity would be increased tenfold, and that the whole school, girls and staff included, would be obliged to 'notice' her. She simply must think out something really good.

Two facts combined to render possible Pip's desire for an 'April Fool' on a grand scale. One was the fact that it was Lent, and Miss Parker was fond of forcing the presence of intellectual or religious lecturers upon bored audiences of sleepy school-girls at any time, but especially during this season. The other was the presence of Uncle Claud in a town some fifteen miles away...

[Briefly, what Pip did was persuade her acting-prone Uncle Claud to pose as Canon of Norwich and offer to give a Lent lecture to the school on 'The Fundamental Differences between Evangelical and High Anglican Doctrines' (a, to me, not entirely arcane subject). His offer is gratefully accepted by Miss Parker, and he duly arrives and gives the lecture, contriving to make his appearance, his delivery (he assumes a lisp) and the lecture's content preposterous and risible. Unfortunately (for Pip) he concludes by letting on that it has all been an April Fool's Day joke, inspired by his great-niece

Philippa Sladen. The episode ends thus:]

Three main results came of Uncle Claud's 'lecture'. Firstly Pip was awarded a Conduct Mark, a severe penalty, and spent the rest of the day in bed bookless, and, at teatime, jamless — to Pip's mind, and stomach, a far more serious penalty than getting a Conduct Mark. Secondly the Very Reverend Humphrey Sladen had cause to feel troubled in spirit, on reading Pip's report. Thirdly Pip again added a chapter to 'Oaklands' history, this time to the knowledge of all, so that she was 'noticed' by everyone, deeply discussed, and became, for the few remaining days of term, the most popular and sought-after girl in her form.

* * *

Although no such incident ever occurred in my schooldays I did enjoy a brief spell of unwarranted popularity after my father once gave a very well received conjuring performance at Stover. No doubt this was at the back of my mind when I wrote this chapter of *Those Happiest Days*.

7

Since my parents were evangelical Protestants, my childhood was dominated by religion rather than politics — except insofar as the two intermingled. However, certain experiences and parental attitudes clearly affected my later life. My mother, who was a dreadful snob (I couldn't join the local Brownies for fear they spoiled my impeccable upper-class accent), was also, no doubt because of her not un-Quakerly Plymouth Brethren background, an ill-defined pacifist. She didn't like my brothers boxing at school (although they did — Keith in fact excelling); nor was she very happy when they joined up in World War II. She herself boycotted Japanese goods when Japan invaded China. Years later, when she had become too much of an arthritic invalid to do anything active for the peace movement, she was nevertheless prepared to wear a CND badge and make donations to *Peace News*. Once when I was quite young — probably about seven — I asked what 'war' was. I don't remember the reply I received, but, whatever it was, I don't think it left me much the wiser. Even so, I must have had some notion what the term meant. The Vicarage walls were decorated with African spears and shields presented to my father by some missionary relative. The handle of one spear that he used proudly to show visitors was covered with gruesome notches, each representing a life taken by the weapon.

When I was eight there came the intimations of World War II — Munich. I accompanied Nanny, who joined the Red Cross, as she went round measuring people for gas masks. When a year or so later war actually broke out I was, as far as I can remember, quite pleased as I expected it to be exciting. I don't know why I should have felt like this: not long before I had been terrified by the possibility of the IRA bombing buildings in Torquay (by then our home-town).

Although straightforward politics did not loom large in my early childhood — not indeed until after I had left school — racial matters did affect me. I seem to have developed a fairly cosmopolitan attitude when I was quite young — probably because my family was rife with missionaries and I attended many missionary lectures and 'magic lantern' (slide) shows.

My parents' views may have been the current, old-fashioned, condescending-to-the-Heathen ones; however, *The Round World*, a children's missionary magazine, was prescribed reading. Its cover design was a large globe encircled by children of all races holding hands. And then there was the famous picture of Our Lord surrounded by many-coloured children.

For a while we had Jewish refugees living in the basement of our large Torquay rectory; consequently I soon learned about Nazi atrocities. Our evacuee from London was a Jewish refugee too; so was a 'cleaning lady' we had for a short time until she, bafflingly, was interned. And my mother ran a Bible class for Jewish refugees which was intended simultaneously to teach them English and convert them to Christianity.

There are one or two entries in my teenage diary which indicate how well aware I was of Nazi atrocities. An entry made in May 1944, when I was a fourteen-year-old pupil at my then school, Stover, runs thus:

...we all adjourned to the hall for a lecture given by an ex-prisoner of war...

Although Prisoners' life sounded grim & the food bad, yet it appeared that it is not quite so awful as I had imagined. I had pictured shootings, floggings & torture as in concentration camps, whereas the chief complaints were boredom & hunger.

The following July my diary contained this entry:

While up at Cheltenham [to sit the Cheltenham Ladies' College scholarship examinations the previous spring when I was thirteen] there had been an exhibition of Nazi atrocities called 'The evil we fight.' Nobody under 15 could see it, & Daddy would not let me try & get in. At this time the exhibition was on in the Gas Works [rooms] here [Torquay], & I went to see it. There is nothing really worth recording about it here except that there were photos & writings about German massacres, atrocities, historical & presentday sayings, youth movements & child training, and immorality.

I don't think I was callous — evidently, for some reason, I had an inkling about what was going on in Germany before the concentration camps were liberated, with attendant publicity, and the war in Europe ended. This is borne out by an item in my diary written when I was fifteen, a day or two before World War II ended, which throws light on some of my general views about atrocities and how to prevent them in future:

Anne & I went to *Laura*, a 'tec film... The News consisted of photos of the living skeletons & dead bodies who had been occupiers of German concentration camps. Having read of so many horrors in books at one time & another, seen horrifying untrue or founded on fact flics and heard so long about German atrocities, I found myself to be hardened against feeling undue horror on seeing this news film & in a way I suppose I felt, & still do feel, being so far removed by circumstances, if not space, from the German atrocities, that these horrors are no more true or actually happening now than events one reads of in fiction or history books. I suppose inevitably many of my generation, in like circumstances, are growing equally philosophical & hardened on the subject of these atrocities. In a way I suppose it is a bad sign for children & young people to be hardened, & yet it may point to the fact that when they are grown up & hold the reigns of government in their own hands, they will be fitted to deal with all wrongs, cruelties & injustices, ruthlessly & with a cool lack of emotion which might go a long way to stamp them out. Perhaps in the long run people hardened against horror are better able to deal with it than the emotional idealists & the less hardened.

One of the chapters in *Those Happiest Days* is revealing on this subject, for, like my later, more mature and better written *Multicolour*, *Those Happiest Days* is fiction, albeit heavily spiced with truth.

At Stover we (and that certainly included me) treated our more timid, ineffective teachers unmercifully. Miss Klempner, a Jewish refugee from Austria, who taught me German as well as French, was the victim of considerable teasing because of her foreign accent. But she was not treated quite as viciously as Old Ash in the story, which, among other things, reveals how basically ambivalent I must have been about our taunting of our feebler teachers, one of whom could quite easily be reduced to tears.

'A Piece of Misplaced Patriotism'
(a chapter from *Those Happiest Days*)

There must be something of a narrowing nature about a girls' boarding school. During term time girls will imagine and do the most peculiar things which it would never enter their heads to do or think about at home, where there are such broader horizons, and so many absorbing interests...

Whatever may be the rights and wrongs of having boarding

schools, it is true to say that daygirls lack that incentive, present among many boarders, to indulge in midnight feasts and bathes. Nor do daygirls, as a rule, become seriously perturbed as to the likelihood of a certain member of the staff being a German spy...

Gretchen Asch, a florid dumpy little woman, with untidy hair, in the early thirties, was a German Jewess from Berlin. Before the War she had suffered. She had been denied jobs, openly scoffed at, and, one terrible day, she and some friends had been rounded up by a mob, stripped, and beaten until their blood ran and they had fainted. Then the War had come, and one day Gretchen came home, after trying to do some shopping, to find that her parents had gone. The old man who lived in the flat above said that the Gestapo had come and led them away. She never saw them again, and never knew that finally their starved bodies helped to pile higher one of the heaps of fleshless corpses in the concentration camp at Belsen. Gretchen herself, together with some friends, after many risks and difficulties, escaped to France in a sailing boat, and then crossed over to England.

For months the word 'England' had, for Gretchen Asch, conjured up the picture of a Promised Land flowing with the milk of human kindness. Somehow, when she arrived there, it just had not been quite as she had hoped and expected it would be. That young curate and his wife had been very good to her, but she had sensed an attitude of latent hostility in the children. Perhaps it was because she was a Jewess, or again perhaps it was because she was a German. Then for months she had not managed to get a job. Nobody seemed to want her — she was just in the way. Finally with joy she had learnt that her application for the post of French and German mistress in a small girls' private school in the Midlands had been accepted.

Again Gretchen suffered disappointment. The children at 'Oaklands' were not like the children she had known in Germany. They would not co-operate; they did not seem as though they wanted to learn anything at all, and they were as

bored and inattentive in lessons devoted to the study of
Goethe's poetry as during those spent in reading the works of
Guy de Maupassant. They were not only uncooperative in
lessons, but they were also thoroughly rude and undisciplined. They threw horrid little paper bags of water called
'water bombs' at each other while she was trying to teach.
They placed drawing pins on her chair, chattered continuously during lessons, and often, on entering a form-room, she
would see conspicuous designs on the black-board of a very
short, very fat person, with a crimson face and wisps of hair
protruding at right angles from its head. Gretchen supposed
these artistic creations were intended both to represent her
and to be noticed by her.

They did not try very hard to make her feel at home at
'Oaklands'. Miss Parker was patronising, the girls, giggling,
would try to imitate her accent and slight grammatical errors,
and even the other members of the staff, although superficially pleasant, were the slightest bit distant, so that Gretchen
did not often like to ask one of them to spend an afternoon
off with her. Sometimes, when the day had been particularly
irksome and tiring, Gretchen would cry a little, quite quietly,
in bed — life might be real and earnest and all that, but it
seemed unbearably hard sometimes.

Pip did not know all this. To her Old Ash (the name
acquired by Gretchen soon after her arrival at 'Oaklands') was
just something that was as stupid and helpless as it looked, just
a person at whose expense she might display her admirable
wit, thus making all the others laugh, and possibly even
drawing forth an enchanting smile on the face of Tessa [the
girl at Oaklands she was in love with]. Perhaps, had she known
Gretchen's past history, and that by drawing cartoons of her
on the board, and in imitating her accent and grammatical
lapses by constantly saying to the others during French and
German lessons, 'You ees all vehry vehry bad children', she
added appreciably to Gretchen's great weight of trouble, Pip's
better nature would have come to the fore, and the display of
her wit during French and German lessons might not have

been so continually evident. She did not know, and so was a source of misery to Gretchen throughout many a forty-minute period.

Finally and inevitably, when the unpopularity of Old Ash was at its height, rumours from a source unknown began to circulate. The chief rumour stated that Old Ash must be a spy, and this for two reasons. Firstly because, when taking prep one night, she had been seen writing a letter which she was illustrating with drawings and plans, that, without doubt, were of great military and strategic importance. Secondly because she was in the habit of flashing her torch out of her bedroom window at night, and so was undoubtedly signalling messages to a fellow spy. These two reasons were to be explained away quite easily. The above-mentioned letter was to one of Gretchen's refugee friends. Gretchen was not a bad hand at drawing, and had illustrated the letter with cartoons of such noteworthy people as Matron, Miss Parker and Pip, also with a diagram to illustrate the small dimensions of her bedroom. The 'signalling' also was easily to be explained away. Gretchen, although a Jewess by blood, was Christian by religion, and a devout one at that, who prayed and read her Bible last thing every night. She liked doing this by an open window, and so, unable to keep the light on because of the 'black-out', she had to use a torch. The torch had a blue glass, and so Gretchen, not considering it necessary to be very cautioius with it, used to wave it around as freely as the spirit, or rather the comfort of her position, drove her to do.

Innumerable 'Anti-Ash' societies came into being, in one of which Pip became the leading light. Most of these societies were formed for the sole purpose of making Gretchen's life a misery to her, but the underlying motive of Pip's society was of a far more dangerous nature — it was patriotism. As soon as a spirit such as Pip's becomes fired by patriotism it will shrink at nothing.

One evening, in one of the bath cubicles, there was a meeting of the 'Anti-Ash Society'. (All but Pip's Society had dwindled in importance, so that by then it was '*The* Anti-Ash

Society'). The members present included Pip, Bob, Val, Chris, and even Tessa, who had descended to earth temporarily to organise the others and have some fun...

Pip's head was in rather a whirl. She was, at that moment, swayed by two strong emotions, patriotism and the desire to rid her country of all its foes, mixed with a fierce longing to impress Tessa in some way. An idea came to her, and one of her dare-devil spasms overpowered her.

They were trying to think out some way of proving the guilt of Old Ash so that she might be dismissed from her post at 'Oaklands'. The thought that if Old Ash were proved to be a spy, she would not only quit 'Oaklands' but also make a rapid and premature exit from this life did not strike them. Then Pip's idea came to her, and she stated her readiness to break into the bedroom of Old Ash at some opportune time, search there for incriminating documents, provided that someone would go with her. Bob agreed to do so, and Tessa arranged when the event should take place.

Thus it came about that, on the following Saturday afternoon, when Gretchen was having her afternoon off, and was said to have gone to see a film in a nearby town, Bob and Pip were to be seen creeping cautiously up the stairs of the Staff Wing. They had made certain that all the staff were either out-of-doors or in the Staff Room before they set off on their patriotic mission. Bob was carrying a tennis racquet, and they were both armed with guide knives, the best weapons they could muster, in case Old Ash should appear bearing loaded firearms. When they arrived at Gretchen's room, Bob 'kept cave' by the door, while Pip, being a German scholar, opened up all Gretchen's drawers and cases, and rummaged among her papers.

From time to time the true object of her investigation escaped Pip's memory, and she became quite engrossed in what she was able to decipher of certain amorous letters from one Franz, until Bob's eager query as to whether she had found anything interesting roused her. The letters from Franz were not the only interesting things she saw. There were some quite good sketches, evidently done by Gretchen, that interested Pip, and from some of her letters from English friends, she gleaned a little about Gretchen's former suffering. Pip was just about to clear up the havoc she had created in the room, after deciding, with some disappointment, that Old Ash was probably not a suspicious character after all, when Bob darted into the room whispering frantically: 'Under the bed quick. She's just coming'.

It was such a glorious afternoon that Gretchen had decided it was too good to spend in the dark stuffiness of a picture house. Instead she took a solitary walk in the grounds, and, on returning, went up to her room to change. It was a Heavenly afternoon, and for once she was able to be quite alone, not having to try in vain to retain order among undisciplined children, nor make forced conversation with the other members of the staff, whose mentalities and ways of thinking seemed so different from her's. She was tired after her walk, and saw the chaotic state of her bedroom with unperceiving eyes. She stooped to take another pair of shoes from beneath her bed. To her horror she then saw that the shoes were enjoying the society of the two most abominable children at 'Oaklands', Bob Collins and Pip Sladen.

While lying under the bed Pip suddenly realised what a worm she was. Those letters had given her some hints about the Hellish time Old Ash had had in the past. There she, Pip, had been, committing the unforgivable sin of prying into another person's drawers and reading her private letters. If she had stopped to think she would have realised that there was not really the remotest likelihood of Old Ash being a spy. Truth to tell she had so wanted her to be a spy, as it would cause such excitement, that she had deluded herself into imagining the impossible. After all, was it likely that Old Ash, being a Jewess, would want to help Germany at all? Was it not far more likely that she herself should have suffered untold miseries? Had she, Pip, thought of all this before she might not have ragged Old Ash so much, and she certainly would not have come probing around in her bedroom that afternoon; but she never did stop to think till too late — at least so they all always told her. Never mind, she would not be such a thorn in the flesh to Old Ash in the future, and she would do her utmost to squash all Anti-Ash Societies.

So Pip thought, but it was too late, for Gretchen discovered them...

Pip never knew that, had it not been for the thoughtlessness of her and Bob, Gretchen would probably not have left 'Oaklands' at the end of term (which was only about ten days distant). Nor did she know that, disheartened by her failures in England, Gretchen sailed for America a few months later, that her ship was torpedoed, and that Gretchen was among those who never reached their destination...

*   *   *

It was not only Jews and their plight that made an impression on me as a child. World War II brought many black American troops to Britain. During the war the Stover grounds were both a secret ammunition dump, more or less concealed by the plentiful trees (a fact which, I later learned, Miss Dence for obvious reasons did not impart to her pupils' parents) and an army camp. Initially, the campers were British soldiers; later they were Americans, both black and white. I remember one day Miss Dence rebuking the Juniors for pulling faces at the black soldiers.

My diary tells more than one tale about my attitude, as a teenager, to foreigners and black people. The first incident related, which occurred when I was thirteen, was perhaps the moment when I became an adult: I had to make a very difficult decision and try, for probably the first time, to put myself into other people's shoes.

In early February 1944 I made the following entry in my diary, which includes details about a typical school day as well as about the incident itself:

...During games commenced the most unpleasant incident in my life, so far as it had gone. I was playing, as is customary, in goal, & Mrs Henderson was taking games. When we changed ends I went down to the end of the field, away from the drive, & on the other side of the fence a black Yank soldier was leaning against a post. C.B., the other goalie, had been chatting to him about lax [lacrosse]. When I took up C.B.'s former position I also passed remarks about the game & then Mrs H came up and said she did not think I had better talk to a soldier, & then told the soldier that she did not think he had better talk to a 'young lady' — me —, though she probably did not use those actual words. Anyway after she had moved off we chatted again — he began I believe —. We moaned at the stupidity of the affair, & he asked whether Mrs H was married — she was fairly waddling under the weight of her impending child. I replied in the affirmative & he said that he thought so. Quite what he meant I do not know. Either he must have guessed that she was pregnant, or else have put down her narrow mindedness, with regard to converse between us, to the fact that she was married & therefore 'stoojy' & full of old fashioned ideas about the propriety of young girls carrying on converse with soldiers. I & others waved to him at the end of games. Going in Mrs H rebuked me for talking after having been forbidden to do so. I replied that I did not intend to cut, or be rude to a Yank, & she said who was I to talk about being rude; but cheeking one's staff [teachers] & people one comes continually in contact with, is quite different from cutting a soldier who is merely chatting amicably on the other side of a fence, & moreover a black stranger to one's land, who is an ally. Mrs H told me to report to Miss D [Miss Dence]. It all seemed so unreasonable & unfriendly that it made my blood, figuratively speaking, boil. During prep I passed notes saying *whatever* happened I would not apologise. I decided that it was more important to be friendly & polite to a black soldier than to obey a pointless command of a school-mistress. I could not go to Miss D until after supper, & she said to me that either I was to promise to always obey anything a staff ordered where the soldiers were concerned, or she would phone up my parents that moment and refuse to take further responsibility for me. I refused to make the promise & then I quitted Miss D's study. I told Ann & Mira what had happened & they tried to make me go back on my word, apparently Ann even cried. Then Mummy & Daddy phoned and tried to do likewise. I returned to Mira & Ann & then retired out on to the roof outside the 3rd form where I prayed violently to be guided into the right course. I spent just about the most hellish night & indeed any period, night or day, in my life. In bed, at one point I as good as decided not to make the promise, but I could not get to sleep for the weight on my mind, & my sleep was troubled and fitful. To put the cap on, Matron even cut my nails before I went to bed. [For some physical — or Freudian? — reason I could not bear having short nails.] After lights I went on the Haytor [name of dormitory] window sill and prayed to God to be shown what to do. I asked for a sign of some sort. Miss D came in & asked if I was asleep, but I was not properly aware of what she said until she had gone. Ann & Mira prayed & talked about it all too, & I gathered later that they were hurt that I did not go & talk to them, but I had not known that they had wanted me to, & anyway it was all up to me to decide what course to take. I went up to the 'John' & read my bible, but it was not until much later, after much fitful sleep — night or morning I do not know, — that I made my final decision which can be summed up by a note I wrote to Mira & Ann next day, which ran as follows:

'I thought for simpley hours last night, & I tried to see the state of affairs from every view point, Miss D's, army regulations, black Yanks' & whether I was just being an idiot and showing off. I decided eventually that I was not trying to show off, but that the whole thing was really on my conscience i.e. cutting Yanks at a staff's orders for no particular reason. From the Yank's point of view, they apparently are breaking army regulations in talking to us, & I suppose these regulations are reasonable as if the Yanks can talk to us at all, then they may one day go too far. Although primarily there may appear no harm in talking ("Familiarity breeds contempt"), & the Yanks, as I said before, may take advantage of this allowance, & although I merely wanted to be friendly & pass the time of day, yet there may be, or will be sometime, weak-minded girls who do *not* merely want to be friendly. Moreover there have to be rules & lines drawn somewhere in every establishment for the common wellfare... Eventually I decided — I tried not to think of it from own point of view, i.e. Cheltenham etc.[1] — and that whether I stayed or went it would make no difference to the principal of the thing. There is wrong somewhere, but it is not the sort that can be righted by my leaving. The real trouble I suppose is the nature & morality of human beings... I thank you, Mira and Ann very much for bothering so much about it all. I do not think I should have if I had been you. I suppose the others know about it all [they did not]. Tell them all this if they want to know. Miss D & the High Command have said all this in different words too.'

Wed: Feb: 2nd. I went to Miss D before prayers. She revealed all her points of view, which I had thought out the night before anyway. Apparently she would have taken similar steps in the case of any soldiers, white, or black. Anyway I made the required promise, to which I had reconciled my conscience the night before for the afore-mentioned reasons... Throughout the morning I felt silent and replied, quite truthfully, that nothing had ensued, to any enquiries about what had happened when I went to Miss D. Later in the day I bucked up however, & during games took part in a fatuous disorganised game of netball — most people played lax — when I was centre v Carter, & we all played the fool, except Maywin & 'po' — who waxed quite ratty when Carter refused to rise from her sitting

[1] I was due to sit for a Cheltenham Ladies' College scholarship examination and afraid that if I were expelled from Stover all future plans for my education would be jeopardised.

position on the netball court. At supper time I was sufficiently recovered from the past events to be able to talk & joke about them with Ann & Mira. I said how light-hearted I felt now it was all over, and they said they felt likewise, which shows they must have cared a good deal about my fate, which is a good thought — I do not seem to have many friends. They said how hurt they had been when I had apparently taken no notice of them when returning to bed from the window-sill, when they were just behind me; however I rectified this matter by explaining that I had not known they wanted to talk, & also their close proximity to me had given me rather a surprise, also I had wanted to turn things over in my own mind. They said how they had prayed for me to remain — a fact of which I was already aware — & that they had come to a decision about me, which Ann said she would impart later. There were oranges at supper, but I ate mine afterwards up in the form room. I danced after supper, with various people including Carter a certain amount, who taught me new steps, & whirled me round until I was all nigh in what I believe is called an old fashioned waltz.

Thurs: Feb: 3rd. The preceding night Ann had brought me a note concerning the decision she & Mira had formed concerning me. It said that they thought that people thought me queer & often did not like me because I was not sufficiently unselfish in small matters, & never went out of my way to help people; but that I would probably give my life if necessary, & that I appeared to think more of the Wellfare of mankind as a whole than that of individuals. Perhaps they were right in a sense, but I should not have thought I was wholly unhelpful to my contempories, I deputise housework and give away sweets when I am sent some. I should not have thought that I was a very unselfish person, but I should not have thought I was especially selfish — however outside opinion is more likely to be correct than mine...

A couple of days later my mother descended on me. My diary account of her visit runs thus:

Mummy turned up, as forewarned, before the end of games. She was wearing a bottle green velvet head-dress like a W.A.A.F. cap, which rendered her rather unrecognisable, and made me feel shifty. She brought a note for Miss D — Miss D out — which asked her to resend particulars about my subjects for the scholarship, so that eventually it was decided I should do German and not bilge [biology].[2] Mummy brought me no eats, & while we walked down Teigngrace drive our 2 sole topics of conversation were, general housing, clothing etc: conditions as regards the impending scholarship; & a long pi-jaw about the Black Yank incident, in which Mummy repointed out all Miss D's points of view, with one addition i.e. the story of my converse might get magnified and so give the school a bad name — which in my opinion might not be a bad thing, as the sooner little schools like this go, the better — this is a rather disloyal & ungrateful outlook of mine. (Could not be bothered to tell Mummy all my points of view. She seemed quite unsympathetic.)

As for my father, it seems in a letter 'he gave me a bit of pi-jaw about the Black Yank Affair, but did not ladel it on too thick.' Peter wrote too: he 'approved my spirit & motives, but deplored my sagacity in the Black Yank business'.

Both Miss Dence and my parents thought my conduct over the Black Yank Affair was just an example of my general bad behaviour, disobedience and defiance. Unlike my contemporaries, they never understood my real motives; and for this I never forgave them. It was, after all, the values my parents had instilled in me that had prompted my behaviour.

[2] When I was twelve I was allowed to choose whether to learn domestic science, Latin or German. I settled for German as it was a living language I might actually use later to help 'build bridges' between the Germans and us after the war.

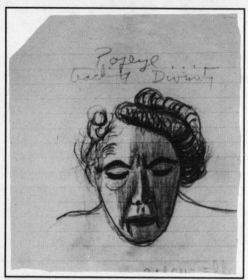

Popeye Teaching Divinity (pencil; age sixteen)

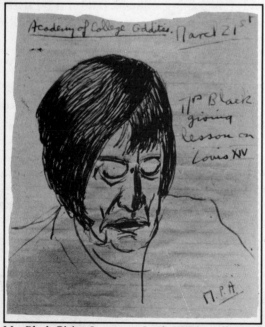

Mrs Black Giving Lesson on Louis XIV (pencil; age sixteen)

8

I became cheekier and cheekier to the teachers and broke more and more rules until finally Miss Dence gave up in despair and about four months after the Black Yank Affair simply expelled me, having already several times threatened to do so. My diary contains a detailed account of my eventual expulsion and what prompted it:

Sat 10th [1944]. This Saturday the 10th of June was the day that Stover & all pertaining thereto began to tumble, (I suppose in a sense, by my pulling), down about me. In the afternoon I went out to play rounders. It was one of those hot afternoons, when, with the sun scorching down, it seems mere folly to stand and melt, feeling dejectedly bored, along with the greater proportion of the rest of the boarders playing a so called game. Meg, Rew & Zena, all apparently felt the same as me, & we were allowed to go & play tennis instead. I found however that it was not a tennisy afternoon either, & suddenly the grand idea occured to me of going for a row in the once-aforementioned boat on the lake.[1] I broached the subject to Zena who 'wasn't having any', i.e. refused to accompany me. I then routed out Meg [member of a different form which had not been thus threatened] & after much disuasion from Roo

& sundry questions from the staff on duty, Miss Wright & the 'chicken' [Miss Checkley], as to what we were doing hovering around not playing tennis or rounders, Meg & I decided to venture off. We spent a pleasant afternoon, but unfortunately we found no boat. I have not time to enlarge greatly on what we did, & anyway we did not do much. Surfice to say that nobody caught us, that we enjoyed ourselves getting muddy exploring islandish places, found a long hissing snake & only encountered one Yank who merely informed us, at my asking, that he had seen nobody around. However it was a fatal afternoon — one of those when I feel imbued with a dare devil spirit, and ready to 'make one heap of all my winnings & risk it on one turn of pitch and toss', for I knew that if Miss D found out it would be sure to mean the sack after all she had said to our form.

This devilish spirit led Meg & I to march quite openly along the main road part of the way, but we eventually returned via the stables, down the drive & back past the Red court. On arrival back Rew greeted us with the uncomfortable news that Miss Wright & 'the Chicken' (& two other staff I later discovered) had been spending the entire afternoon searching for us. Nothing happened however until just before tea, but then the two staff on duty summoned us, & just outside the staff-room — the door being open — enquired how & where we had spent the afternoon. I tried hedging with truthful excuses, but eventually gave it up as a bad job & admitted that we had been out of bounds, whereupon Miss Wright said it would be her bounden duty to send us to Miss D. I pleaded that she might not as it would mean the curtailment of my time at Stover, & she told us to go & have tea.

[1] A potentially heinous offence — at that stage we were barely even allowed out of the school buildings on our own because of the soldiers, never mind going for a row on the lake in the grounds. Furthermore, my form had recently been warned that, as we were all so badly behaved, any one of us who committed a further misdeed would be instantly expelled.

After tea — forgetting completely to wash up — Meg & I wandered in the garden, & then Miss Wright came out & said it was no good, but we must go to Miss D at about a quarter to 7, not just then as she was resting. Meg then drifted off & I wandered around in a state of solitary & mute abandonment. I have never prayed so hard & earnestly as I did at odd intervals that evening not to be kicked out when Miss D knew the worst, but in my heart I saw how foolhardy I had been that afternoon, & that considering what she had said, Miss D was not very likely to let us off. Also I felt that as I had been foolish, knowing the penalty if my foolishness were discovered, that I deserved to suffer my punishment. I wandered around back — I had been on the Terrace wall by the 'Temple of Love' [one of the follies in the grounds] — to by the Annex tennis courts where darning was in progress. Nobody as then knew of the plight of Meg & I except for Zena, Rew, 'Tickles' & perhaps 'Stinks.' Ann came out & said that as I had forgotten to wash up, a nice little pile of plates had been left for me to deal with. I retired gloomily within to fulfill my task, & at the same time tried to be pleasant with the Bickles, Mrs kindly informing me about paints obtainable at Woolworth's. When I went out again people remarked on my douer countenance, & Biddy [the girl I was in love with and who knew I was because about a year ago I had, with great trepidation, brought myself to confess my feelings to her] rather unkindly remarked that it was not worth looking at. I felt hurt at this & at people's apparently callous (as I felt it) attitude. If they did not know what had happened, or rather what was going to happen, then I felt they should have known something was wrong. Booker had arranged to play tennis with me, & I resolved to stick to the plan, partly as it would help to pass the long evening. I told her what had happened, what would happen in the future, & probably eventually in the further future, & grumbled about Biddy's untactful remark. She sympathised. There were no courts available except for the Annex ones, & I did not feel I could face playing on them, while in all probability an audience would watch & pass witty remarks.

In the end I went & did some of Meg's darning for her, & then we wandered around. Throughout the evening we were both experiencing most acute 'dentist pains', which obliged us to relax our industry every now & then & lie on the grass with acute agony written on our faces, & sometimes to even laugh rather wildly at some mild joke. Over & over in my brain the words that I felt Miss D would say repeated themselves: 'Well Pat you know what that means...' or, 'I am afraid that means...' & then I would try & delude myself that she might complete her sentence with the words, 'A conduct mark', but all the time I felt that her sentence was liable to end differently, & yet I could not bring myself to believe that a few days might see my quittal of Stover Portals for ever. The evening seemed eventually to drag to a close, & after having changed, Meg & I appeared waiting outside Miss D's study door — nobody was in the room. I had felt quite ill with dread when we knocked on the door, but when we discovered that we would have to wait, a lot of my dread left me. As we waited nearly every boarder passed by, coming in & up from the garden. It was interesting looking at the expression on each face that saw me. Some smiled sympathetically, some looked curious & others passed by quite disinterestedly.

At last we heard the fateful step of Lydia [Miss Lydgate, the deputy head] descending in a horribly brisk & businesslike way... she arrived. 'The chicken' had reported us & so we did not have anything to say, & she, Lydia, did not have much either. She said that she had been informed of our misdeed, she asked, I believe, where we had been, said that Miss D would deal with us on Sunday or Monday, that she supposed we knew what it would mean, & that if we had anything to say, we were to say it. Having nothing whatever to say I fled upstairs, leaving Meg saying she did not know what would happen, but then Meg was not in my form & had not been told by Miss D that there were certain people she 'would not hesitate' to send home at the next provocation. I told Ann & Bella [Mirabel, sometimes called Mira, sometimes Bella] what had happened, & I suppose rumours flew around as they do in communities. Anyway at supper Mary D wanted to know the outcome of my visit to Deedle's[2] study, & when I made out that nothing had occured, she looked incredulous.

I could not think what to do after supper, & in the end retired to the music room & tried to sooth myself with the aid of the piano & slow renderings of Handel's 'Largo.' I felt awful in bed, not knowing what my fate would be, & wondering whether to go to Miss D the next day of myself & promise to break no more rules that term. I caught Biddy gazing rather intently at me some of the time. Meg seemed tolerably cheerful before bed, but in bed she began to cry & so went to the 'John' where Roo soon followed her. Meg told me later that Roo was a brick with her that night. I did not fall asleep for a long time & my slumbers eventually were troubled. Unfortunately I was unable to genuinely cry in bed that night or the next. (It occured to me to wonder & enquire of people whether it would be worth while to send my clothes to the laundry, but in the end I did send them, partly as even then I could not quite believe that I was liable to be turfed out in a day or two.)

Sun June 11th. In passing I will remark that that morning Mirabel was removed to the San with chickenpox — very bad luck. I felt grim all through breakfast & made no attempt to keep Connell amused with conversation. After breakfast, up in the form-room, I felt composed enough to continue drawing a face I had begun the previous morning, (the face of a glamorous pin-up girl I copied in pencil from a 'Yank' magazine. It went through various stages before completion: (a.) a stage when people said it was good since glamorous faces were not my style, (b.) when it was, as I then supposed, finished, looking much too long & old, (c.) a rubbing out stage

[2] Miss D was variously known as Miss D, Deedle, Deedle Wee and Peddle — the last partly because her initials were P.E.D. and partly because she was a pianist.

— which was the stage I was at on that Sunday morning — & (d.) the final & quite satisfactory stage.) This drawing turned my thoughts & made me feel better. Suddenly brisk business-like steps sounded outside the form room, 'Lydia' bumped in, looked all around the room before her eyes alighted on me under her nose, & said, 'Er Pat will you go to Miss Dence in ten minutes.' I continued to draw in silence — a silence had fallen on the whole room — after 'Lydia' went. When the time came to go I was not feeling as troubled as might have been expected, as I had just about completed my drawing & was feeling quite satisfied therewith. I went to Miss D in her study, & it all fell out as I had dreaded, but whether she actually said, 'Well I am afraid that means...' I cannot be certain, but assuredly she did not end what she said with the words, 'A conduct mark.' What she said amounted to the fact that whatever promise I made, & she did not doubt but that I could keep my word, it would be impossible for me to remain at Stover after what had been said to our form. That if I stayed she, Miss D, would be despised (or words to that affect), that she had given the matter due consideration & was very sorry. I returned blankly to the form room, first telling Meg what had happened. (Meg did not go to 'Deedle' until Monday, & as her form had not had solemn warnings, etc, she got off with a conduct mark [the receipt of three such marks was supposed to result in expulsion] and a promise not to break rules.)

It was just time for service, but for a few minutes I went to the window & looking out on the sweep of drive & across the garden by the cedar trees & Annex Courts to the Red Court & practically empty camp in the distance, I shed a brief tear or two that I would not be wandering, sketching, playing tennis or biking in it again. Connell bagged me a place at the service, but I felt rather sorry that Biddy did not. After all it was my last Sunday; I should never again after that day be able to sit by her, & as I had bagged her places the Sunday, & indeed many other Sundays, before, she must have known I would like to have been by her. Anyway enough of that now. After the service I told people generally in the dressing room what had befallen, & I will say this, blaming nobody for it all but myself, except Miss D in that she had said how insolent I still was in lessons & how in her lessons she had often wanted to slap my face. People who had also been with me during lessons professed no knowledge as to why she could have ever been overcome with such a malicious feeling, as they could not think how I had been in any way provoking. (To my pleasure Biddy grumbled about my departure, saying I was needed for the 3 legged & tug-of-war on Sports Day.)...

After lunch my feelings underwent a reversion, & quite suddenly I felt I did not mind a bit. I thought I should probably remain until half term & therefore be here for Sports Day, also I thought that I should be able after all to go up for Peter's Speech Day, & later the gladsome thought that in all probability I should be able to partake of lots of strawberries at home struck me. I ran down the passage wreathed in grins, which Lydia, standing near, must have seen and been amazed at. I felt comparatively happy all afternoon, to people's astonishment & grinned whenever I looked at Meg. I suppose this was because I felt so relieved to be no longer in suspense.

I wrote a short very penitent letter home & then drifted into the garden with Meg as pre-arranged. In the end I sat apart under the 2nd cedar tree copying, without a vast deal of success, a photo of Leslie Howard, as Meg seemed surrounded with other people. Biddy, Booker & Connell played together, & I felt a little sadly that I should have liked to spend my last Sunday afternoon with them, some of the friends of my form. I had a bathe, feeling quite cheerful, doing a weird semi-successful treble dive with Carter & someone else, & yelling out quite happily that I should not be able to do Bronze [life-saving medal], & therefore feeling rather glad as I should not be obliged to undergo that nose, eyes & ears filling occupation of learning to duck dive...

After tea Meg & I wandered until service again. We talked about many things & I felt sad again. I said that even then I was thinking more about leaving Biddy & about the usual lack of friendleness between us than of expulsion... Then too I said how there were very few people who I felt would miss me. Meg tried to console me, said there were & that she would miss me & could scarcely believe I was going. Among other things I said that I thought God perhaps made me break rules — not the Devil (if there is such an one) — in order to try me in some way or for some set reason.

At evening service I again did not sit by Biddy — by whom I do not remember. I do not remember much about those 2 last services — during the first I was fighting back weepy tendancies some of the time. I know that we did not sing any especially favorite hymns of mine, but that we sang psalm 91 (I believe) in the morning & the Walmsley Magnificat in the evening... At supper I caught Mary D & Shirley eyeing me a little quizzically. After supper I went on with Leslie Howard's portrait (?). I do not recollect feeling too awful in bed. I felt that after all I would probably stay until half term & therefore had time enough to get cut up on Thursday night, moreover the awful suspense of the yesternight was over. I read — as I had not done on the previous nights, — & fell asleep at a fairly normal time gazing across at Biddy as usual.

Monday June 12th. When I was down from washing in the D.S. Lab', Matron told me to collect all my things ready to pack, as, to my shock, I found I was to go that afternoon, & to my wrath it appeared that Mummy was coming over. I went upstairs feeling rather desparate, & in the form room cupboard, with 'Filly' [Zena] standing by and Pat Wheeler in another part of the room, I cried briefly. On Saturday I had not been able to find any relief in the solace of tears, & on Sunday I had only cried just before morning service & a very little, quite quietly, in bed on Sunday night. I am afraid for pretty well the rest of my time as a Stover pupil, I went around with a strained expression, & that once more I gave way to tears in the bathroom before Zena in break.

Before prayers & during the first 2 periods I packed. People were all kind and helped to bring down my things, &

Connell helped me in the customary heavy, or not weighty enough, task of closing down my trunk. I did all my little last odd jobs, & then went to maths, the 2nd period, & did nothing. We had French that morning, did Maupassant & sat in odd places to share books. We had German in the garden, & scripture last period for which I deemed it prudent, although I was going in the afternoon, to look over the prep. I remember it was tested in class, & I drew a very poor map of Palestine... The staff were pleasant, Lydia included, & Matron even made complimentary remarks on a painting while I packed. After eating in break I went on the games field with Meg, where Sports practice was in progress. Meg told me about her interview with Miss D, & how she could not believe I was going. It hurt rather to see Biddy doing 3 legged with Zena, to see people practicing for races in which I should not run, & to know that I could never possibly run white-clad up the steps under the portico to receive the coveted 440 yards cup. After scripture at the end of the morning Miss D called me back to say goodbye. She said how sorry she was about the way things had mapped out, & wished me good luck. She seemed really cut up & wore an odd expression as she kissed me goodbye...

I had to wait a long time outside Miss D's study & as I did an endless stream of girls passed by going upstairs. It seemed somehow to me as if all the girls I had ever known at Stover went trooping past, as in 'Goodbye Mr Chips' just before the old man's death a whole long stream of all his old pupils seemed to go by him for roll call again. Evidently my fate was known generally, although I had only had occasion to tell one person, — Nicol — outside my own circle. Anyway nearly all who passed by wished me luck or stuck their thumbs up. Then Lydia came out of the study with a list she had just written out of all she thought it would be expedient for me to revise for history. She gave me my identity card etc., & was 'jolly decent,' to put it school girl fashion. She explained what she had written, wished me luck, told me to let her know if I were ever muddled, & made no catty remarks, only murmuring something about having been a 'silly little ass.' I found difficulty in keeping complete command of my voice as I spoke (in fact I don't think I did).

After this Connell came out & as usual pumped up my tyres. (For some obscure reason I always seem to be quite incapable of performing this operation myself with any success.) Biddy had borrowed my byke the day before, lowered the saddle & omitted to raise it again. Something had gone wrong with a screw, & Mr Coles (who to my mild astonishment professed blandly to have ridden on my byke & approved thereof) spent a lot of time trying to right matters without success, so that I gloomily foresaw myself peddling home with a low wobbling saddle. However he righted it eventually. I felt inwardly impatient at having to wait while Mr Coles tinkered around, as I particularly wanted Biddy to cut my nails for the last time before my departure, because I might have got a chance of saying some sort of goodbye, & there would be no more opportunity after 'Rest'. Such was not to be — I mean the nail cutting stunt — as the 2nd bell for prep went before I arrived back in the form room. I had 'Puck of Pook's Hill' before me in preptime. I did not read much, however.

Ann wrote me a short farewell note, I wrote one back, & Carter asked me to write sometime. Now that the time of going was so near — I was to go about 3 — a lot of my dread fell from me... Suddenly I decided to write to Biddy whether she hated me or not. Accordingly, as once before I had written Biddy a rather pathetic note just before she was expelled[3], so then, just before I was expelled, I wrote again rather miserably. I said I knew she hated me, but that I had always wanted

---

[3] She herself had a year or so before been briefly expelled — for no very specific reason — then allowed to return as she was a Londoner, the blitz had resumed, and her mother had besought Miss Dence to let her return as no other school would take her — Miss Dence agreeing, after first solemnly informing the Seniors that she was doing so as, on this occasion, she was putting 'humanity' above 'morality'.

her for a friend, that I would write & hoped she would do likewise. I ended by wishing her luck in winning the diving, swimming & length under water, 3 legging it with Zena, & punctuating her essays, (Miss Mitchell used to continually find fault with her method of doing — or not doing — the latter.) Biddy laughed when she got to the end of the note. I found later that Ann, thinking the note was for her, had begun reading it & had been surprised on reading, 'I know you hate me...'

I sensed Biddy then writing back, & it seemed a long epistle, but eventually it turned out to be just over a side of rough book paper. Later she went & searched for something on her shelf, & a perfect shower of notes sailed at me from Ann, with words to the effect that Biddy was hunting for a Shakespeare, & then that she was borrowing Roddy's, in order to give me a quotation. We laughed. Suddenly footsteps sounded along the passage and Miss Mitchell entered saying, 'Will you come now Pat.' The dreaded moment had arrived. I arose, delivered 'Puck of Pook's Hill' to Carter, & bade the form farewell. I quitted the room. Biddy went out before & was waiting on the other side of the door. She gripped my hand, pressing her note into it at the same time, & said, 'Goodbye Pat, & good luck.' It might have been my imagination but I thought her face was a bit flushed. Her voice & manner were different from usual. She seemed, in that short space, older, or anyway as if it were her real self talking, — as often I am sure it used not to be. (She herself once admitted that although she laughed at Booker, yet she was never genuinely amused by her.) I rather think Biddy wanted to cry. Perhaps she was genuinely sad then that she 'should behold my face no more.' She did not return to the formroom but went to the 'John'.

Miss Mitchell told me to go & put any loose articles in the case outside Miss D's study & then wait there for Mummy. She then kindly said how sorry she was that I was going as I was a good worker. I poked my head around Lower V door & said goodbye. They all bade me farewell & Meg said she would write. I then collected my things together from the dorm...

While waiting for Mummy to emerge form Deedle's sanctum, I perused Biddy's note. I shall always keep it & so there is no need to enter deeply into the contents thereof. She said that underneath (here again verifying my theory that often she had worn a sort of superficial personality) she did not dislike me. She tried to show why she had been hard on the outside. She told me to cheer up & she sermonised quite nicely even bringing in God. She said she would write when she had time i.e. not just then, told me to think kindly of her, & she would of me, & rounding all off with a quotation from Macbeth Act I Scene VII: 'Screw your courage to the sticking point & you'll not fail.' Actually these words were said by Lady Macbeth when egging on her husband to kill Duncan. Whether Biddy was expecting me to culminate all my crimes by finally comitting a murder, I do not know.

Mummy emerged from the study. She was clad more smartly than I had seen for a long time. Her voice was quite naturally rather cold & hard. She, I & Miss D went through the Hall — poor Hoopy trying to have a violin lesson the while — dealt with the luggage, & I brought around my byke. To my horror I found that a taxi was taking my luggage to Newton station, but not Mummy, by whose side I was doomed to have to cycle to Newton. I seemed to sit for ages, but at last Mummy and Miss D came out and we went, I bicycling miserably along beside Mummy who walked rolled away from Stover for ever into different roads of life & a larger world beyond.

I do not remember much of that painful journey into Newton. I remember feeling foolish bicycling along beside Mummy past the day girls at the bus stop, & feeling foolish at the set off as when Josephine Kellock &, I believe, Sheila Holman, called out goodbye near the swimming pool, I yelled back some misplaced remark about good luck to Vicky house on Sports Day — they were both Maryites as I remembered afterwards. Mummy & I did not talk a great deal as we went along. Some of the time we were both trying with difficulty not to cry, & almost each time I encountered Mummy for the rest of the day she looked weepy...

It appeared that during Miss D's discourse with Mummy she had said she was quite sorry to lose me & had grown quite fond of me. I suppose all that was 'eye wash' to try & console Mummy, as it differed almost entirely from anything she had ever said to me. Also she had said I was a hard worker with a 'thirst for knowledge', — the first not wholly true I am afraid, — but that actually my last exercise for her had not been as good as usual — I had got 6 out of 10 & no dirty comments, quite tolerable. To me she had said that my work had suffered from my insolence in class, in which case it must have suffered ever since my 3rd term at Stover, when I stopped feeling new & timorous, & incidentally when my work underwent a deffinate change for the better after my first 2 shocking, as regards work, terms. Anyhow during my 2 latter terms at Stover I had dropped being insolent, as even my friends vouched, almost entirely in lessons.

At Newton Mummy & I parted company, she catching a bus. Bicycling on alone, I let off pent up steam by putting my back into the exercise. At Kingskerswell the bus caught me up, & from thence on, nearly all the way to Torquay, we raced. I went ahead at each bus stop, & was then overtaken before the next was reached. Eventualy I easily won, & sailed puffedly and triumphantly down past the station into Torquay... At last I reached that grim chocolate coloured pile of building which is my home, & my first step was to go & see if the gooseberries or currants were ripe. Needless to say they were not & so my thirst remained unassuaged. I then repaired homewards. As I stood diffidently in the conservatory doorway, hearing Daddy's approaching footsteps with dread, the dim hall looked cool & gloomy, & I realised that when I stepped in I would once again be absorbed into the not wholly gentle clutches of home life.

Daddy arrived and I grinned weakly. I was led off to the study — my byke still in the road — installed on Daddy's knee, lectured gently, & then dismissed with a kiss like a little girl. I forget how the remainder of the day passed, (nothing further happened of importance,) except that I played the piano a bit & had a total of 3 more short lectures from Gran & Goody [my grandmother's companion who lived with us in our large, chocolate-brown painted rectory for a number of years]. During Gran's 2nd one just before I went to bed — her first one was a mere nothing — I was tickled by her foolish way of putting things, saying my brothers would be grieved with their sister etc & unfortunately I showed some amusement. Gran was naturally peeved & said she did not think I was a bit sorry for all that had passed, but when I explained that my mirth was a reaction after all the preceeding dreadfulness, we were reconciled. I seem to remember more kissing from Gran, & I believe from 'Goody' too — most damping mentally & physically. Anyone would have thought I had done something rather wonderful, from the number of people who carried out this wet operation on me. Of course there had been no question of kissing Biddy, the one person by whom I should love to have been kissed. I suppose the idea never occured to her, & if it did, was turned down as likely to have been unpleasant to both parties concerned.

* * *

Many years later I learned that actually my parents had both considered my expulsion very unjust. Unfortunately I had no inkling of this at the time; on the contrary, I was made to feel very much in disgrace for quite a long while.

Lying was, in my parents' opinion, 'one of the greater sins' (indeed it was one of the sins that as a child — and well on into adulthood — I almost never committed; I think this applied to my brothers too). Their efforts never to tell an actual verbal lie sometimes, however, got them into tangles of deceit. Once after we had returned from a Gilbert and Sullivan opera and my grandmother (who considered anything remotely theatrical the epitome of wickedness) asked where we had been, my mother, in order to prevent a mother-in-law volcano eruption, promptly (and wisely) responded: 'We've been to a sort of secular oratorio.'

After my expulsion from Stover they told puzzled members of the church congregation that I was back home in the middle of the summer term in order to do my School Certificate examinations at the local Grammar School. The Churchwarden's wife (who had public schoolboy sons) was not convinced. However, in a sense it was true — I did, a month or so later, do the examinations at the local girls' grammar school. Later I learned unofficially (Miss Dence evidently did not want me to have the satisfaction of knowing this) that I had come top of the Stover candidates. This was surprising as I was not usually top of my form (of which I was the youngest member), but as a rule came third or fourth. Probably I benefited from several lesson-free weeks during which I could concentrate on revising for the examinations. And my parents sent me two or three times a week to a 'crammer' — an elderly ex-schoolmaster who helped me considerably over mathematics, my weakest subject.

9

When I compare notes now with contempories about our schooldays I realise what an extraordinary, almost St. Trinian's-like school Stover must have been. Years later a colleague who had gone to a nearby school told me that when her school played away matches against Stover the team was always instructed not to stay on for 'match tea' as the Stover girls were 'such a bad influence'. I didn't realise at the time what a peculiar school Stover was (although I later discovered that Cheltenham Ladies' College was much primmer and duller). There was probably more overt homosexuality at Stover than is usual at 'nice' girls' boarding schools — there was certainly more than in any of my Cheltenham houses where I don't recall there being any. I remember a tom-boyish Stover VIth former (who features in my diary) who was ordered to become a 'weekly boarder' as she was carrying on with one of the juniors and it was less easy for the affair to proceed if she were home at weekends.

Then there was Rew (or 'Roo') and the 'Yanks'. Roo, a late-comer to Stover, was decidedly more sophisticated than the rest of us. Not content with a lesbian relationship with her 'Best Friend', she also got involved to some extent with the American soldiers (by then white) camped within furlongs of the school who were soon watching her almost all day through binoculars. She would get her friends (including me) to play tennis with her on one of the more remote courts, which was nevertheless still just 'within bounds'. We would deliberately hit the ball out into the bushes, where Roo would then go, ostensibly to look for it, and collect notes, packets of chewing gum and once a two-shilling piece left there by her American soldier boyfriend, whom she also contrived from time to time to meet. Just what he got in return I'm not sure. And she would blow goodnight kisses from the form-room window to the row of soldiers sitting not far away gazing at her through binoculars. Soon half the form were following her example. Then we started trying to have morse code conversations with them from the form-room window during (unsupervised) prep-time, when we should have been studying hard for our impending School Certificate exams. But perhaps the American soldiers' morse code was different from the English Girl Guides' one we knew: we never managed to communicate properly.

One of the imaginary episodes in *Those Happiest Days* among other things depicts this bizarre situation. After I had written the novel my father got it typed for me but insisted on my watering down the franker, more shocking details. But somehow I managed to retain the original, which is the version reproduced here.

'A Military Event'
(a chapter from *Those Happiest Days*)

Towards the end of her time at 'Oaklands' three facts combined to cause quite a memorable stage in Pip's career. One was the fact that, because of the imminent invasion of France, almost over-night, a fungus of tents, containing a certain portion of the American Army, appeared in the grounds of 'Oaklands'. The second was the fact that Pip was growing up. She was fourteen, and, as Miss Parker believed in 'pushing on' her more intelligent pupils, she was to take School Certificate at the end of that term when part of the American Army chose the grounds of 'Oaklands' as a camping site. She had weathered many storms, met quite a lot of different people, mixed with girls older than herself, and consequently was, in some ways, old for her age. The third fact was the arrival of Vivienne Best.

Vivienne Best was the type of girl who would be described by any sane headmistress as a Bad Influence. There were ways in which Miss Parker was not a sane headmistress, and, although she often professed to have the ability of seeing considerably further than the end of her nose, she revealed an extraordinary lack of observation in some respects. This was proved in that Vivienne Best, who should have been ejected piecemeal from 'Oaklands' almost as soon as she arrived there, was allowed to have a peaceful and normal departure after failing School Certificate, while Pip, lawless, rude, and often positively ear-splitting, but not really harmful to anyone's morals, was compelled to have an abrupt termination to her 'Oaklands' career.

Vivienne Best arrived in a shining cloud of Bad Influence that promptly brought her general popularity. Her hair, hanging shoulder-length, was a mass of tangled hair-dresser-made curls. She had those things that, to a plain and ordinary school-girl, are the essence of glamour. She had photos innumerable of members of the opposite sex, with a story attached to each photo which, in some way, revealed the passion with which the photographed one regarded her. She used powder and lipstick in moderation from first to last without anyone breathing a word in protest. (Perhaps, as she was never without lipstick, Miss Parker failed ever to realise that her lips were not by nature two shades brighter than anyone else's). Her clothes had that something about them which made them different from, and more elaborate than other people's. Yet she was not good looking. To many members of her own sex she was not even attractive, although, for some obscure reason, she could charm all men.

Viv (for so she was immediately called at 'Oaklands' where every effort was invariably made not to call people by their full or real names) to start with did not exude Bad Influence of a very dangerous nature. Apart from the Boots and the Odd-Jobs there were no males resident within two miles of 'Oaklands', and so there was nobody on whom the girls could vent their newly awakened interest in the opposite sex aroused by Viv. As time went on, and no interesting men or boys appeared, Viv began to feel the restraint upon her sexual emotions too strongly, and so had to make the best of sentimental scenes with other girls. These scenes came to be generally known about, and, at first, were laughed to scorn. But the 'pash' system was still prevalent at 'Oaklands', and gradually other such scenes began to take place. Of these, although not of their originator, Miss Parker became aware. Once she discovered two girls, one a junior and the other a contemporary of Pip's, embracing each other in a bath cubicle at an hour when both should have been in bed. She took measures to try and stamp out this 'silly sentimentality', as she called it, but she was worried. Things like that were not good in a school, but unfortunately they did not disappear over-night.

Pip was not affected by this wave of sentimentality. She was not very demonstrative. She disliked kissing people on the whole, her parents included, and was inclined to be blunt and matter-of-fact. She was not the sort of person on whom girls openly had pashes, as she was noted for scoffing at such sentiments. Nobody would have guessed that she, figuratively speaking, worshipped the ground that Tessa Trelawny walked on, nor that she was capable of feeling at all emotionally disposed towards her. Yet it was so; for long before Viv's arrival at 'Oaklands' Pip had often thought what bliss it would be to throw her arms around Tessa's neck — provided Tessa responded warmly. But then again she was not sure because Tessa was not a 'Kissy lovey dovey' sort of person, and if she had been Pip would never have thought twice about her.

Then the Yanks came, and Pip did come under Viv's sway.

The school became encircled by tents up to three feet from the edge of the games field. The inevitable happened. Viv was scrutinised through binoculars at almost all times when she was visible during the day. Then she tried signalling to the soldiers. Other people also were, or thought they were, gazed upon amorously through binoculars, and they too tried to signal.

One evening, when they should have been soberly meditating on such mystical and elusive subjects as cosines, quadratics, and 'cum with the subjunctive', practically the entire school certificate class (who had unsupervised prep) did their utmost to signal morse messages to a group of soldiers gathered at the edge of the camp. This became the regular way of spending evening prep-time in the Upper Vth — small wonder that five people did not pass School Certificate that summer, a greater number of failures than there had been for ten years. Unfortunately some of the prefects found out what was going on, and it was only after promising not to do any more signalling to the soldiers that the Upper Vth evaded the dire penalties they would have incurred had the matter been reported to Miss Parker.

It would have been impossible for Viv, with such an attractive horde of virility encamped almost on her doorstep, to have treated it as though non-existent. She took to sending little notes to one particular soldier, from whom she received amorous replies, usually with some chewing gum or 'candy' enclosed. A certain conveniently placed laurel bush acted as a letter box, and other girls, with less doubtful and suspicious characters than Viv herself, acted as postmen.

Gradually other girls began to correspond with particular soldiers also, but the business became rather risky as the laurel bush was too exposed, and so Viv thought out a fresh way of corresponding. She used to go and play tennis with friends on a court that was practically invisible from the school and on the precincts of the camp. They would purposely send balls off the court, so that, in going to fetch them, they could collect little notes and packages deposited in the grass by the soldiers who were lurking in the surrounding bushes. It was at this time that Pip was always to be found in Viv's company.

Pip had often felt slightly jealous of Val Morgan and other girls who boasted of their devoted boy friends. She herself rarely had dealings with anyone of the opposite sex other than her father, uncles and brothers, but now, here she was encircled by soldiers who seemed ready to fall for anything in skirts, no matter what it looked like. What fun if she had a Yankee boy friend. How delightfully shocked they would all be at home if they knew. She was fourteen now, and all the others — at least all of them that counted — seemed to have boy friends, so why shouldn't she too? To obtain a boy friend all she had to do was to go around enough with Viv, who was incessantly watched by the soldiers, and one of them would undoubtedly suddenly notice her.

She did go around with Viv. Together they blew kisses to the soldiers from the form-room window every night. Together they played tennis as scantily dressed as possible, Viv wearing shorts and a floral patterned sun-top, and Pip, shorts over a bathing costume. The hoped-for happened. Little packages and amorous notes began appearing for the 'Brunette', which, as Pip was dark and Viv fair, were obviously intended for the former. She wrote replies that were practically dictated to her by Viv. Her cup was almost full.

The only flaw in Pip's contentment at that time was caused by Tessa. Pip really was not at all in love with any soldiers, and she was only carrying on with them because it seemed an exciting grown-up sort of thing to do. Truth to tell, although she did not admit it even to herself, Pip did not much like the look of her particular soldier, who was called Johnny. He was smallish, dark, and rather oily looking. She still worshipped at Tessa's shrine.

Tessa herself regarded these goings on with the American soldiers with disdain. She was older and wiser than the others. Had there not been such a large VIth form, and had she been a little less dreamy and detached, she would probably have been made a prefect, but as it was she had to be content with captaining her form and various tennis and lacrosse teams. She herself was not without interest in boys. She met many of her brother's friends, whom she liked — some of them rather more than 'liked' her. Francis Pengelly with his red hair and black eyes excited her rather. She had even let him kiss her that night last holidays at the FitzRoger's dance. American soldiers are of a different calibre altogether from public school boys and young subalterns or undergraduates, and it troubled Tessa slightly to see 'quite decent kids' like Val Morgan and Pip Sladen becoming 'thorough little flirts'. She derided. She called Pip a 'ruddy little fool', and then she retired and left them to carry on as they would. She did not know that a heart to heart talk with Pip could probably have revolutionized her. She only knew that Pip, to all outward appearances, was about as obstinate and pig-headed as she could be.

One day Pip received a note from Johnny suggesting a meeting in the dusk some evening. Things were going a bit far, so she wrote a note of refusal, this time undictated by Viv. Matters grew worse. Pip began receiving letters that were, to her mind, quite indecently amorous, in which Johnny implored her to meet him alone some time. She sent a crushing reply, and then sent no more notes. But Johnny did, and his tone began to grow slightly threatening — if she would not comply with his wishes she had better look out, as he quite definitely intended to have a solitary meeting with her some time. Pip ignored his notes.

One evening she played tennis with some friends on the court close to the camp. When it was time to go in Pip stayed behind to search for a ball she had lost somewhere in the long grass. It was a mellow summer evening, and everything seemed silent. Pip's thoughts, if concentrated on anything in particular, were about her chances of coming second in the halfmile race on Sports Day.

She did not hear a slight rustle in the bushes close by. Suddenly, as she was standing gazing aimlessly into nothingness, an arm slipped around her waist. She felt herself swivelled round, and gazed into the face of Johnny. He gave her an ugly little smile, and squeezed her with his arm. Pip furiously demanded to be released, and tried in vain to free herself from his grip. Then she saw the utter hopelessness of her position. She did not cry out as nobody was near enough to hear. Half stupified she heard him say: 'So I have got you at last, eh? I told you I should in the end, honey.' She continued to struggle feebly. He squeezed her more tightly and said: 'Steady, now. No use wearing yourself out, baby. I only want you for a little while.'

Pip knew well enough what he wanted, and in a moment of time she had a mental picture of all the horrible consequences that might follow. She might have a baby. She might die having it. She would have to leave school, and would probably never be able to get a job or anything.

Perhaps she would have had a baby, and her life might have been ruined or else have come to an abrupt end had she not remembered something her cousin Helen had once told her. Johnny carried her off into the bushes. Realising the futility of further struggling, she remained passive, paralysed with hopelessness, in his arms. Then she remembered. Helen had said: 'If ever you get into difficulties with a man, pretend to feel sick and he will leave you in disgust.'

It was worth trying. Pip began to choke, gasp, and gurgle rather unrealistically. Johnny had a hand inside her blouse and was pawing her. His face was greasy and pimply. Beads of sweat stood out on his brow, and his breath smelt of beer. Quite suddenly Pip genuinely was sick. Johnny was taken by surprise. This was not what he had expected. He had seduced and forced other girls, but they had not been like this. They had struggled and screamed and he had enjoyed controlling them and making them do as he chose. Instinctively he let go of Pip and drew away. She sprang up, and, overcome with sudden rage, kicked him in the face with all her remaining strength. She never knew whether she really injured his face badly or not. She then ran back to the school (far faster than she ran in the halfmile race on Sports Day).

When she went indoors they all noticed her flushed and dishevelled appearance — but then she had been playing tennis, and presumably had run back as fast as she could by way of practice for Sports Day.

Two days later was 'D' Day. The camp emptied, and Pip saw Johnny no more, although, for many years, her dreams were sometimes haunted by the memory of the pressure of his hands on her body, and his amazed and horrified expression just before she planted her foot in his up-turned face. But she had learnt her lesson. She never again made herself cheap to any man, and in later years was famed for her caution in all her dealings with the opposite sex.

* * *

In fact nothing of the sort ever happened to me. My closest encounter with any of the American troops is described in my diary entry for Thursday April 20th, 1944. It was the school holidays and I was fourteen at the time.

The diary describes how I cycled off to spend the day with schoolfriend Ann, who lived in a village about fifteen miles away. It was, as I put it, 'A wizard day'. My account of our afternoon cycle ride up on to Dartmoor includes a comment on my reactions to the ubiquitous American troops:

'As usual we encountered thousands of Yanks in lorries & camps who whistled and hallood so much at us that I answered in the same way. One was most desirous for me to stop & talk to him, but that was no especial compliment however as the Yanks make eyes at & bee-lines for anything in skirts.'

The following is my account of the trip home:

Going out of Newton a lorry full of White, hooting Yanks passed, one of whom chucked a packet of something, probably chewing gum, at me. I did not demean myself by stopping to pick whatever it was up, but when the lorry was out of sight, being fond of chewing gum, I returned in search of it, but my belated efforts were fruitless, someone else had got there first. Nearly all the way home I had a nigger escort. [I was quite unaware then that terms like 'nigger' and 'darky' were grossly insulting.] While I was riding along I passed a Black Yank on a byke who said, 'Cean I ride alongsida you?' I ignored this request, but the darkie pedalled vigorously up to me & repeated himself. I was vague & diffident but when he pointed out that there was road between us, I agreed. After all it was the Newton Rd & it was just this sort of cutting of Yanks which I had abhorred the term before at school, so that in the end I had my nigger companion all the way to Tor Station. We talked about various odd things. He told me his name, which was quite incomprehensible. I did not let out such information as my surname or adresse, which might have later caused trouble. He was amazed that I said I had cycled all day, & was even more so when I evinced a rather untruthful desire for a bathe. Apparently he had worked formerly in an air-craft factory, I believe in New York, & preferred civil to mylitary life. He did not seem to know where his camp was. He could tell I did not understand his dialect well as I kept asking him to repeat what he had said. He was rather shockedly surprised when I said I disliked alcohol and smoking, but said he would give me some 'Ceandy' & 'gum' — (he never did unfortunately, because I believe he thought I did not want it). He said he thought I was old for my age & even got as far as calling me beautiful & making remarks like 'Its nard offen I cean ride wi swee lille geal like you.' When I said I should not be able to meet him again, he seemed hurt & indignant, also when I said I must not be seen in the town with him, & he could not understand when I tried to explain rules of social etiquette such as girls not being allowed with strange soldiers. I lied that I was going back to school the next day so that I should be able to comfortably get out of having to decline further offers of his future society. Of course I did not tell Mummy all this, or I should never probably have been allowed byking alone again, & I did not even tell Peter of this novel experience for several days. That night in bed I felt happy at the combined experiences of the day, but rather sorry that I had not been given the 'ceandy' & gum & that I had not gone & smoked in a pub with the Yank as I doubtless could have done — it would have been a novel experience. Anyway I felt I had had an interesting ride back from Newton, partly because it had been so unladylike & shocking — just supposing the Wesmacots had seen my riding along with a black!

10

My lengthy, detailed, at first usually daily-written diary does not include very many direct references to The War, which, for the most part, simply sidles fairly unobtrusively into my blow-by-blow account of each day's events. Much of the diary is about quite trivial matters (which seemed important at the time): my weekly marks; what we ate for supper; lacrosse and netball matches... However, it does here and there combine accounts of everyday matters and my current activities and preoccupations with descriptions of the bizarre wartime situation I was then in at Stover — which, although I did not know this at the time, very nearly had to be closed down for 'the duration'. For instance, in my entry for Sunday May 28th, 1944 I wrote:

Before lunch I went apart & began a sketch over in the Red Court direction. However I was not moved of the spirit to continue, & instead spent the afternoon trying to paint the swimming pool from the diving board — a very difficult task, as although the water was clear & green — as then unbathed in — yet sometimes when I looked at it, it was a mass of little rainbow-like orange and blue lights. Mira being absent, Ann came and sat by me on the diving board steps & did a pencil sketch of the school. (That afternoon a sergeant snarled up on a motor cycle, saying that we could no longer sketch the school.)... After tea Ann coached me at tennis over on the Red Court... We had another service in the evening. I bagged Biddy a place by me at the morning one, & felt sorry as she did not bag me one in the evening. I painted for the rest of the day.

Another 1944 entry runs thus:

29th-9th. Another period of school life with sundry fresh happenings to record... The roads were blocked towards the middle of the week & so buses, 'Iggledy' [Miss Igglesdon, the art teacher] & daygirls from Torquay were unable to come. On Sunday night — in actuality the small hours of Monday morning, I was awoken by a crash of bombs somewhere in the not extreemly close vicinity. Without waiting for fire whistles we all got out of bed & made for the cellars, where so much noise ensued that any further bombings were almost inaudible. We remained in the cellars for, I suppose, about an hour, during which time I partook of 2 mothy-tasting biscuits, wondered which angle I should lean in, & contemplated the unusual bizarre sight of Lydia minus specs & in night attire. I gathered later that various towns along the coast, Plymouth, Dartmouth & Torquay had been bombed. I felt a little worried about the state of the 'Chocolate box' [our family home] & had sundry different rumours imparted to me concerning the damage done in Torquay. It was said at first that there had been little or no damage caused as all the bombs fell on open ground, but this rumour was soon found to be untrue. There were bombs down by the harbour, behind Queen's Hotel & by the semi circular china shop, also up Babacomb & Ellacomb way. On Tuesday the 'Home Front' phoned 'Deedle' to say that a small bomb (Mummy said later that it might have only been a shell) had fallen just below the garden in Thurlow Rd. I gathered later that the hill up to the house had prevented much blast & that only a small amount of glass was smashed, & that apart from that, all else that had happened was (a.) Some heavy books had crashed to the ground (b.) Goody had gone from the shelter to the house in the middle of the raid to fetch Gran's shawl & had imagined she heard china crashing — presumably the books & glass — & had felt mortar fall on her shoe, the latter altogether unlikely, & (c.) Mummy & Goody thought they heard cries of distress, but on examination for a distraught & helpless person, found nothing...

One new development at that time was a friendship founded between Rew & the Yanks of the camp. It began by the latter watching Rew all day through binoculars...

On Saturday the 3rd Mummy phoned up while I was standing deepfielding (?) on the rounders field, to know if I could go out with her. Off my own bat I agreed to meet her at the end of Teigngrace Drive & then go to Newton & have tea with her there. It was all a bit tricky, letting Miss D know that I had blandly given myself permission to go out, & then being lent thermoses etc which I had no intention of using, & trying not to let Deedle know that I was going to Newton. However all want off alright, & in spite of the fact that I lost my identity card & permit, which I found the following day, I was able to get out alright, as the sentry, instead of guarding, was showing the Howels, — likewise 'out' that afternoon — photos. The following day Sunday, it rained, so that there was no sitting around in the garden. Some Yank sailors came & our form drew lots as to who should show them round. I drew a lot, but not being wildly enthusiastic gave it to Roo who was. I sketched from the dressing room all afternoon.

I must mention the important political events occuring about this time. On June 5th we heard that Rome had at last fallen into Allied hands. The next day, 'D Day', the invasion of Europe began, & we saw the Yanks marching out of the camp to embark — although actually a great many had already gone. We were allowed to hear the King broadcast at 9 that night, & the VIth form & we were allowed to hear the news & etceteras afterwards. Of course everyone promptly began making war maps & invasion diaries by the dozen, although I cannot say I did. Somehow the war seemed to be brought much nearer than before when one could hear distant bangs & saw men actually marching off to war & death. Although the opening up of the 2nd front had an exhilirating feeling — things going back to normal & the troops disappearing — so that one felt the end of the war might be in sight, yet there was an unpleasant feeling at the back of one's mind that the Yanks, who a week or so previously had perhaps been watching & hooting while one played tennis on the red court, might at that moment be lying bleeding, dying, or blown to bits on some beach along the coast of France. Concerning the military side of the invasion I shall write little as there are plenty of others to do so, & anyway I do not remember all the involved details. Let it suffice to say that all the primary war reports were glowing, making the whole show appear a walkover. Later however it appeared that it had not all been quite such easy going, & that at one place on the coast of Normandy, the Allied forces had only advanced 100 yards after a day's fighting. About this time I really felt that to be a journalist might be my vocation. Before I had thought of nothing much seriously — the idea of being an M.P. had just *crosssed* my mind.'

11

I didn't actually know the facts of life until I was eleven or twelve. The lavatory at home was known as 'the place we don't speak about' — even though my brothers and I strip-washed together. I knew that kittens came out of cats and babies out of their mothers, but not how they got in or where they came out — except that in the case of cats it had something to do with liquid passing from the Tom to the female. When I questioned my mother about all this, she replied: 'You don't need to know about that yet, dear — not till you get older.' So I had to acquire the information I wanted from my better-informed schoolmates. Fairly soon after learning the 'facts of life' I learned a lot more besides. One summer holiday Sunday evening when I was twelve (considered too young to accompany the others to the evening church service) I was reading the Bible when I came across the word 'whore'. I looked it up in the dictionary and learned that it meant 'prostitute', which I in turn looked up. Then I caught sight of a book quite prominently displayed on the bookshelf in the study of the vicar in whose house we were staying; it was entitled *Prostitution in Europe*. I was soon engrossed in it. Later I remarked to my parents that the vicar had some very interesting books. 'Oh, you mustn't read any without asking first — just like at home,' they quickly replied. They were too late. And before long I knew all about lesbianism too. Some of the stories we invented and told in the dormitory after 'lights out' (talking 'after lights' was deemed a grave offence) were quite disgustingly — and realistically — pornographic. And they were about homosexual as well as heterosexual behaviour.

Biddy was the first person I fell deeply in love with (I was twelve or thirteen at the time). Later, when I was a student, one or two young men cropped up, briefly and on the whole unsatisfactorily; I soon lost all interest in men and fell in love with women again. We had a lantern lecture on sex one day towards the end of my schooldays at Cheltenham Ladies' College. Afterwards we were invited to ask the (woman) lecturer any questions we liked in confidence. At that time I had erotic feelings about a contemporary who was currently my closest friend. I was worried about this because, now I was seventeen, I felt I ought to have stopped having crushes on girls and should be getting interested in boys. When I told the lecturer about my anxiety she was deeply shocked and quite nonplussed.

As is clear from my diary, I had what was, at Stover, known as a 'pash' on Biddy; but my feelings were, I'm quite sure, different from most of the 'pashes' the other girls claimed to have on some person or another. For one thing, most of my schoolmates had 'pashes' on teachers or much older girls — prefects, games captains... Biddy, however, albeit some two years older than I, was in my form. She came to Stover after I did and when she was a New Girl (by which time I myself had settled down and become reasonably happy at Stover, even though lacking a Best Friend) we were, briefly, simply quite close friends. (Later on Biddy commented once or twice on how nice I had been to her when she was new.) However, I was soon replaced as her Best Friend by Mirabel, whereupon my feelings about her (Biddy) changed. I badly wanted her to be my Best Friend again, and this profound wish rapidly turned into a 'pash' (which I kept secret from everyone, including Biddy, for a very long while). I fell in love with her.

Three quite different sorts of love/liking relationships seemed to prevail at school — anyway at Stover. There were 'pashes' (or crushes) that one had on an older person, often a teacher. These feelings were evidently either genuinely, semi- or quasi-amorous and were very seldom reciprocated in any real way. There were occasional genuine lesbian relationships. And there were Best Friends relationships. The last, with their attendant squabbles and jealousies, somewhat resembled marriages, even though they were for the most part quite platonic. Such friendships might be disrupted by 'adultery' and culminate in 'divorce', after which a fresh 'marriage' took place. There was apt to be considerable partner-swapping. Although such relationships were platonic this did not mean that the 'adulteries', 'divorces' and changing friendship patterns (sometimes a veritable jigsaw) did not cause considerable misery at the time to those concerned. I am not sure I ever had one single Best Friend at either Stover or Cheltenham — anyway for any length of time. One or two of my diary entries are quite revealing about all this and my thoughts about the matter.

On 20 January 1944, the first day of the spring term (Biddy at that time still expelled from Stover), I wrote:

People did not seem, to start with, as lively as usual, & the whole time I felt something missing — of course Biddy had occupied a good deal of space. She had written a letter to the form in which she deplored Miss D's methods, said she had liked everyone, & especially thanked Zena, Joanio & myself for helping her when new. She sent a letter to Meg in which she said she especially liked to get letters from her and me [although she evidently seldom got round to answering mine — the diary is full of lamentations over yet another non-appearance of a letter from her]. She had composed a poem called 'To my friends' the theme of which stated that she hoped to meet us again. It was depreciatory of Stover. The friends to whome it was sent were Mira, Booker, Ann, myself, Connell & Meg. My greeting with Miss D was unsatisfactory. She extended her hand for my ration book etc. & not realising this I proceeded to shake hands. Ann bagged me a place at supper & seemed friendly. Mira did not particularly. She explained that Miss D had blown her up the preceding term for dishonesty coupled with slack work. Everyone talked after lights. Mira went to Ann's bed.[1] I did not talk or want to, but I felt jealous of Mira being with Ann. She, figuratively speaking, got Biddy from me, & now it looks as if she will pair off with Ann, who I like. I felt miserable because of this, & absence of Biddy. Cried inaudibly for a bit. Everyone talked & story-told for ages, & so I did not fall asleep until about 11.30. and also felt it, in my case, unwise to break the silence rule even on the first night.

A month or two later I wrote gloomily:

2 facts spoilt the rest of the day: (a.) the fact that Ann & Mira seemed very thick & were putting heads together about staying in the hols; (b.) Ann's brother Keith had apparently remarked on my plainness — a disconcerting thing to be told only partially counteracted by the fact that Mrs B. had said I looked striking & Ann had said that I was. [It is clear from other entries that I myself didn't think much of my appearance.] In bed I felt rather dismal as originally I had been friends with Biddy, & then she had gone with Mira, & I had felt jealous ever since. Realising I could never be friends again I almost paired off with Ann who had finally gone with Booker. Then the term before there had been Mira, and I was naturally wretched when she had returned to Biddy, & this term I had really

---

[1] This did not mean that they were having a lesbian relationship — friends often broke rules by chatting to each other in one or other of their beds; we were sent to bed unbelievably early — at 6:30 pm until we were twelve — an exception being made in my case as I was academically ahead of my age-group hence had much prep to do. And World War II 'double-summer time' meant we were in bed hours before sunset during the summer terms.

thought I would have Ann & lo' Ann & Mira now spend half the night in each others' beds. I wondered what would happen next day when Biddy [now just returned to Stover, her expulsion having been rescinded] & Ann would both want to go with Mira, as we were to be allowed in the garden again. After supper I sought an outlet to my sorrows on the music room piano...

My next day's entry runs thus:

Eventually Mira went with Biddy in the garden & Ann tacked on to me. We were allowed nowhere hardly except on the terraces[2], & Ann & I sat by the wall. I took my diary, but did not write much as I talked to Ann about friendship muddles. Later Zena came by us & I read my book. Ann had said that the 3 people she liked most here were Mira, Zena & myself. I do not think she can understand the workings of my mind in the least as she said she did not think I liked anyone much. I hastened to disillusion her, & said that the people I liked were Biddy, her, Mira & Zena. As a whole it was not a particularly satisfactory afternoon, as I knew she was wishing she was with Mira the whole time. At tea I felt rather hurt (I do not think I showed it) as Ann said to the table in general that she had been frankly bored until Zena had come along. [On a previous occasion she had flatteringly said I was one of the two people who never bored her.] During bible class Zena & I went to our usual place in the window. Zena slipped off to the 'John' during the hymns, thus causing suppressed mirth. Ann & Mira sat together & poor Biddy sat looking lost, in another part of the room. I felt sorry for her as I could imagine what she was feeling like, & I believe some of the time she was nearly in tears...

[2] This was because of the war and Stover's current somewhat strategic position; on one occasion Miss Dence even informed me that, for security reasons, I couldn't finish a small oil painting I was doing of the back of the school — I had to finish it off later from memory.

In bed that night I went over the Stover friendship problem in my mind. Booker & Carter seemed quite happily saddled together. Meg nominally had Zena, but went with Rew. Connell drifted between Meg & Biddy. Just the same intricacies appeared to be arising with regard to Ann, Mira & Biddy as the previous term with the same people, only myself & not Ann. I wondered how they would work it out, & prayed that it might turn out alright. Eventually however I came to the extreemly satisfactory conclusion that I did not care a 'tinker's curse' what happened to any of them, even Biddy, & that the following sabbath I should be quite able to dispense with Ann's company for the sake of Zena's or just my own.

What a cat's cradle... A somewhat earlier diary entry expresses my then-held views on Best Friends:

During the morning I did prep in a vague sort of way, had my hair cut and washed, & read part of a conversation note-book which Ann & Booker had kept up the preceding summer [when they were Best Friends]. I gleaned various pieces of information about matters not concerning me, & some that did e.g. that although Ann had 'liked me most in the form *at one time*', yet she would never want to be 'B.F's' (best friends — not bloody fools). Anyway she seems to be more my friend now than anyone else, & anyhow I do not hold with 'B.F's', little compacts, notes, secret societies, & the like — they always seem 'to end up in tears' or at any rate quarrels. If you are friends with somebody the wisest policy is just to drift along with them without bothering to write notes saying you are going to do so.

It is clear from different diary entries that my teenage views about 'pashes', sex, boys and men were somewhat confused and contradictory. On 6 April (when I was just fourteen) I wrote this account of a day out during the holidays with Peter which reflects quite a different attitude to the American troops to the attitude I had to my black cycle-ride escort a few weeks later:

Glorious day again after a series of mediocre ones. In the afternoon Peter & I biked off in a vague & leisurely way. We pondered on going to Haytor, but ended by bicycling as far as Bovey. The whole route seemed either to be lined with Yanks, or to be occupied with processions of Yank vehicles — lorries & 'Jeeps'. I was disgusted at the way in which almost every Yank who passed hooted & made remarks at me — British tommies did not seem as a rule to take quite such an unholy interest in one... On the roads we found strips of silver paper, dropped by 'Jerries' to prevent radio location.

And my views on *Men Only* etc. are quite interesting:

After supper I did prep, looked at sundry magazines labelled 'Men Only', 'The Nation's Humour', etc. I must say that if the 'nation's humour' only amounts to sordid, sexy jokes, and photos of half nude women, things must be coming to a pretty pass, as the jokes were not even amusing or particularly clever.

And clearly from an entry made at home that summer I would, in theory at least, have liked to have a boyfriend:

3 tall youths in mufti looking about 19 passed by. They looked at me & one turned & winked. Afterwards it struck me what fun & how comparatively easy to be flirtatious, & how I should like to see a few more of the opposite sex outside my own family circle. It seemed strange to have anyone British, i.e. not in Yank uniform, looking twice at me.

Biddy (pencil; age sixteen)

The Fairy Ship (pencil; age fourteen). 'Highly commended' in the Royal Drawing Society Wartime Children's Competition, 1944.

12

But it was girls, not boys, I was really interested in, and one day I confided in Peter about how I felt. I found the conversation both reassuring and interesting:

Jan: 10th Mon....: I told him about girls' pashes, for one thing, & he told me about boys' equivalent, i.e. sexy attraction to a younger boy, this state of mind I believe he said was known as 'homy'. He said he was inclined to approve of co-ed schools, as there would be none of these unnatural feelings there. I felt inclined to agree...

Although I had some idea about what went on at boys' schools (Ann, who also had a public schoolboy brother, was quite a mine of information on this), it was comforting to learn that Peter was in love with a fellow pupil at his boarding school just as I was with Biddy. Keith was less helpful. When he wrote to me from India (where he was in the army) for my fourteenth birthday he invited me in a kindly, if somewhat avuncular, way to feel free to ask him any question I liked about anything — sex, religion or politics. Foolishly I took him at his word and wrote back asking for certain details I was not quite clear about concerning buggery. He was deeply shocked and in his reply said young girls of my age shouldn't be interested in such matters.

I did discuss 'pashes' in general with my mother one day — not that she had any idea of the depth and nature of my feelings about Biddy, nor that I had a crush on her at all. Much later on in fact, when Stover days were over, I had great difficulty persuading my parents to let Biddy come and stay as she was deemed to have a Bad Influence on me. Indeed it emerged that this entirely erroneous belief (if anything she was apt to be rather didactic towards me) was shared by Miss Dence, who imparted it to my parents; and most unfairly it was partly what led to her temporary expulsion from Stover. Very reluctantly I had to show my parents one of Biddy's rare, somewhat sententious letters to me before they would consent to have her as a guest. The conversation with my mother prompted some general reflections on 'pashes' in my diary:

While washing up supper Mummy & I discussed 'pashes'. I said they were not really any more feeble or ludicrous than the equivalent feelings of a boy. The silly part is when people talk a lot and giggle about them. Biddy once said to Mira that if you have a genuine pash, you do not talk about it much. She also said 'pash' was an ugly word. I think it has too wide and vague a meaning, as the hero worship of a little girl, & the more sexy feelings of older girls are both called by the same name, & therefore seem on a par. Besides, I believe some people only like, or pretend to like someone else, & yet it is still called a 'pash'.[1] I suppose all this is due to the fact that girls always have any type of 'pash' on those older than themselves, whereas in the case of boys, the little ones may hero worship older ones, but an older boy feeling sexy about a younger is naturally different, which in actuality is, I suppose, the case with girls,

[1] I myself simulated a couple of fairly improbable 'pashes' — mainly as a joke, although I am not sure that the subjects realised that my apparent adoration was bogus.

only they never feel impassioned by those younger [not invariably true, I much later learned].

Over a year and several 'pashes' later I wrote:

In fact in rather a vague & abstract way, as I have only seen her once before although I have heard about her since, E. [name omitted; she was one of Keith's first girlfriends] has always been a kind of goddess to me in the background — being pretty, having boy friends & having been a head girl etc. [I was then fifteen, she nineteen and an Oxford undergraduate.] She has not fallen from her pedestal. It is odd, all the different kinds of feelings you can entertain about different people, all of which contain some sexy sentiments & all of which would be classed at Stover [by then I was at Cheltenham] under the one word 'pash'. Biddy is the person I have been craziest over & yet I saw all her faults (at least I think I saw a good many) & did not even admire her in many ways. There are others I have felt keen about but the 'pashy' feelings have dissolved as I either became naturally friendly or fresh interests pushed them out. Not many of these 'pashes' have been objects of my admiration. Usually the fact that it is difficult or impossible to be friendly with these girls breeds the 'pash' feeling, but in E's case I probably would not especially have liked her had she been unfriendly & the mere fact that she was friendly made me feel fond of her. If I ever marry I wonder what my exact feelings towards my husband will be.

Actually, after my very brief heterosexual phase was over, the men I have been fondest of and have got along best with have all, I think, in some remote way reminded me of my brother Peter — long since dead. Although Biddy was not the first person about whom I had passionate feelings I had never before been fully conscious of their physical nature: that in addition to being in love emotionally I was sexually attracted. Clearly, from a number of my diary entries when I was thirteen to fourteen, I was aware of this in Biddy's case — for instance, the following account of a conversation I had with Meg:

After supper Meg & I wandered for ages in the garden... I told her all about my 'pash' on Biddy & how I often felt sexy about her. In return Meg told me that sexy & rather immoral relations were sometimes set up at night when Rew came into her bed. We commiserated together, & I tried to dissuade Meg from carrying on, but, as she pointed out in different words, I was trying to cast the mote out of her eye with a beam still in my own i.e. I wished Meg would not let Rew come & be lovey dovey, but given half a chance, I would have been — or felt I would have been — violently passionate with Biddy. Of course talking all about it (& Meg was the most sympathetic person I told) [for the most part I tried to keep my feelings about Biddy a secret — it wasn't the usual sort of 'pash'] stirred it all up more than ever in my mind, making my feelings unendurable at night as I lay looking at Biddy longing to spring over to her & fling my arms tightly about her. One night shortly after, I felt like this so badly that I muttered to Ann what I was feeling like. She was rather scornful I think, & said that a short time previously Biddy had told her she hated me. At this information all my passion ebbed out. I cried noiselessly in bed & did not fall asleep for sometime that night.

I rounded off my diary account of a day in January 1943 (when I was thirteen) thus: 'Felt very much in love with Biddy. Looked at her photo in the moonlight', and the following night: 'I began telling myself stories about Biddy coming at night to the dorm: to comfort & calm me when ill...continued stories of Biddy to myself...';while a slightly later entry runs: '...told myself sexy, lovey-dovey stories about her'. I arrived back at Stover from Cheltenham, after doing the Ladies' College scholarship exams, feeling both excited and anxious because Biddy too would have just arrived back after her temporary expulsion. However, according to my diary account, she 'just said, "O hullo" & later was generally pally with Connell & completely ignored me, so that I felt hurt...' But a couple of days later things went better: 'In gym we played netball... I played centre, & Biddy played against me. I played quite well I think, better than Biddy I am glad to say. I think she must like feeling that I love her, as she put her arms round my neck for the ball on one occasion.' She was then gratifyingly complimentary about my letters to her and said 'I was the right person to keep a diary'.

Sexual jealousy too emerges in the diary. On one occasion I wrote: 'In bed I felt acutely jealous of Meg & Connell — who were consorting with Biddy... I wished that she would come over to me or else that I could go into bed with her.' The story of one day at about the same time ends: 'I became overcome with sentimentality, & sexy feelings for Biddy that night, & envied Ann when Biddy twiddled her naked about with her arms round her [Ann had no particular feelings about her]. Usually I prefer Biddy clothed to Biddy in the nude, but that night I thought her figure looked quite reasonable. I wanted very much to hug her, as I often had during the daytime when sitting close to her sharing books.' And a bit later: 'I would have liked to have kissed her good night, but opportunity did not offer as she was giving Ann & Booker end-of-term baths [not an untoward activity — we were very free and easy about dressing, undressing and bathing in front of each other at Stover] & anyhow I doubt if I could have if it had come to the point.'

Another night, 'After the bell had gone Biddy went & "snoozled" in Ann's bed. I felt extreemly envious, as there is nothing I could like more than for Biddy to come & "snoozle" down with me in bed, but she probably thinks I should not like it, as generally, I think, I show her a pretty implacable countenance. Anyway she thinks I am an aggressive personage, quite anti kissing or any sentimentality or affectionate friendliness, also I do not suppose she would even want to come & tease me in bed.'

Finally I was 'in a green hell of jealousy & unhappiness' when it emerged that Ann 'liked Biddy & had begun to realise what I saw in her, & that she [Ann] had invited her to stay.

Somehow this made me feel jealous and long to see Biddy. I, who for getting on for 2 years had terribly liked Biddy & would have loved to have had her to stay, or to have stayed with her, had somehow never quite been able to invite her, & Ann who had recently come rather to like her, but who had been quite indifferent about her for ages just invited her to stay all in a moment & that was that. Moreover I thought Biddy was sure to accept the invitation as she had always appeared to be friendly with Ann even when the latter did not especially like her, & often had not seemed at all to like me. It did seem hard & rather unfair for no particular reason, & I felt wretched all day. A day or so later I decided I would damn well ask Biddy to come to us after or before being at Ann's. I would probably, I felt, revel in having her once the ice was broken, & if not, if I felt perpetually shy & awkward, well it would not be for long anyhow.'

Mainly unsatisfactory and unfulfilled though my feelings for and relationship with Biddy were, making me decidedly unhappy for a year or two, the diary, in addition to revealing this, does include one or two accounts of blissful moments, for instance the following passage:

In gym time we were weighed & measured... While awaiting my turn I flapped at the 'Prune' [on whom I pretended to have a 'pash'], & Biddy, who also pretends to be deeply attached to this person, tried to prevent me, holding on to my hands. When I sat on the form next to 'Prune', Biddy came & sat on my knees, & when I continued flapping at the 'Prune', drew my arms around her waist & held on to my hands to stop me doing so. Seated with Biddy on my knees & my arms around her waist, was, I felt, rather an awkward position, although about the pleasantest I could be in. Wisely — so that people should not look & talk as I sensed they were doing a little, — or unwisely — I might never again be in quite such a pleasant situation, therefore why not make the most of it? — I djsengaged myself from hanging around Biddy's waist, she still held my hands however.

On another occasion: 'There was a fire practice that night just as I was about to doze off. I sat with my head against Biddy'. Next day: 'Biddy was friendly in gym even calling me a "little thing" — a phrase of endearment usually reserved only for Ann or Booker.' And another time: 'That night, when asleep, the whistles went — it was about a quarter to 12 — late — & as Miss D. was in pyjamas I rightly surmised that it was not a [air raid] practice. We had been summoned down because "Jerries" were buzzing in the vicinity. Nothing however occured. I went "routing out" in Leighontor [name of dormitory] & became seated next to Biddy in the cellars, where we stayed for about an hour. I tried to doze on Biddy's shoulder, & later she laid her head on mine. Gone were all my thoughts of coldness to her [intermittently I strove, unsuccessfully, to dislike her], I just loved her & loved her head on my shoulder, or leaning against her'. Yet another time I wrote quite bluntly: 'I had felt quite sexy as Biddy had held me steady while Babs did my profile.' And again: 'Biddy came over to show me something concerning the prep. I was seated at my desk. She came behind me & put her arms around me to reach my history book. Her soft body pressed against my head & I could feel her heart beating...sentimental slush!'

It was a long while before Biddy completely fell from her pedestal, even after Stover days were over. When eventually she stayed with me and my parents on one of our summer holidays our relationship was at first awkward and strained, but, clearly, after she went I missed her badly.

I had one or two other brief, insignificant 'pashes', but my next major one was on Phyll, whom Biddy described to me before I went to Cheltenham (where Phyll was a pupil) as she had once been at school with her. Apparently she was good at tennis and music (at which I did not myself excel), and not, in Biddy's opinion, my type. This both roused my interest and was a challenge, so I looked out for Phyll with interest when I went to Cheltenham. She proved to be a goddess; furthermore, being in a different house from me and although, like Biddy, older, in a lower 'year' [form], a tantalisingly remote goddess. While Biddy (as I was all along aware) was somewhat lumpish and not especially beautiful or gifted, Phyll was slender and attractive as well as being good at games and musical. My first diary reference to her and the feelings she evoked in me runs thus:

Phil was at Bredenbery & Biddy told me to look out for her. She is attractive, & very musical & gamesy, & although only a U.C.3, head of lax & music representative of Sydney Lodge. Whether I have ever exchanged one word with her or not I do not know, but I have a strange feeling of heroine worship from afar for her as she is all I shall never be — musical, gamesy & attractive in a way I shall never be. I shall talk to her about Biddy next term. Last term more than ever I felt ambitious, longing to do well in everything & make my name resound in Coll', & somehow after I noticed Phil R. — towards the end of the term — I felt more ambitious — to be in Coll' teams like her, a leader in the house as she must be, & as outstanding at art or work as she is at music.

I started to write poems when I was at Cheltenham. I wrote three sonnets to Phyll, managing to 'post' the first two to her anonymously via the internal College mailing system, supplying Meg's address for her to write back to if she wished. She never did. The sonnets show how I felt about her.

The third and most competent of them was written when I was seventeen, about a year later than the first two. Like the first, it is less about Phyll herself than about my feelings towards her.

To Phyllida (summer 1947)

I see you drawn in patterns by the trees
Whose shadows quiver in an April breeze.
I see you in the pebbles smooth & cool
That line the glass-green shallows of a pool.
And when, at night, I hear the moaning wind
Your voice is mingled with it in my mind.
The scent of grass beneath the morning dew
Is but a wafted memory of you.
So pity me, that in what place I be -
In stifling classroom, neath a rain-soaked tree,
'Mid heavy dust of sweltering summer streets,
Or snow that sweeps the hills in shining sheets -
It is my fate that I can ne'er be free,
But, framed in every scene, your face must see.

Phyll remained a remote figure for most of my time at Cheltenham — unlike Biddy, who at Stover had been close. Eventually, not long before I left Cheltenham, I summoned up my courage and did an extraordinary thing: with parental consent I invited the goddess-like Phyll, whom I scarcely knew, to stay for a week during our family summer holiday. Amazingly, she accepted the invitation — only to become a temporary 'girlfriend' of Keith's on arrival...

Tessa in the following chapter from *Those Happiest Days* is a sort of amalgam of Biddy and Phyll — at least as I viewed and felt about them. Although fiction, the basic story told in the chapter is true: Biddy, Booker and I did once go for a wickedly illegal, nocturnal, mile or so's walk to the lake in the Stover grounds, the dénouement of the adventure being very much the same as Tessa and Pip's in the story. The chapter also echoes some of my diary-expressed views on schoolgirl friendships, 'pashes' and the like.

'Tessa, and a Nocturnal Escapade'
(a chapter from *Those Happiest Days*)

Next term Tessa came. She was Pip's friend for the space of three weeks — at least, looking back later, Pip liked to think she had been. For three weeks she found in Pip quite an amusing companion, as she had a ready wit — often revealed at the expense of others — and was quite interesting to talk to. By the end of three weeks she had discovered that Chris Melville was the person whom she really wanted for a friend.

The system of friendship at 'Oaklands' was not unlike the game of international politics on a small scale. You joined forces with someone for a week or two, a term or two, or perhaps even a year or two. Suddenly you found out how uninteresting your friend was, and how much more desirable was the companionship of someone else's 'best friend'. Bitter scenes ensued. Erstwhile inseparable friends were found wandering forlornly alone, little notes were sent hither and thither, surreptitious 'confabs' took place, and the affair formed the chief topic of conversation while it lasted.

For a year and two terms Val Morgan and Chris Melville had been 'best friends', then suddenly Val grew tired of Chris and came to the sad conclusion that she was rather a 'goody-goody'. Chris sensed her attitude, was hurt, and the two took to snapping at each other. The final rift came one day when Val was expatiating on the 'smashingness' of Martin Kennedy, a sixteen-year-old school friend of her brother's, and produced a photo of him, and a ring, set with a heart-shaped stone, that he had given her. For no apparent reason Chris suddenly burst out and said:

'You and your dancing and boy friends — I'm jolly well sick of it all. Anyhow I bet he doesn't care two hoots about a little twirp of thirteen like you'. She slammed out of the room, and the former inseparable friends were seen no more in each other's society. Val found that Jill Franklyn was as interested in horses and dancing as she was. Chris found the advances of the new girl Tessa Trelawny not unwelcome.

Until Tessa ceased to resort to her company, Pip did not greatly value her friendship, but, as soon as she paired off with Chris, a feeling of possessiveness came over her, and she desired nothing more than to regain the friendship of Tessa. With pain she saw Chris bagging places at table for Tessa, and with bitter jealousy she saw the two going off together in the garden on Sunday afternoons. She had not even got any other particular friends on whom to fall back. The fact that for the rest of her days at 'Oaklands' Pip never really wanted to be great friends with anyone but Tessa prevented her from ever forming any other long-lasting friendship. She rubbed along pretty well with most people, and had spasmodic friendships which led her to pour forth her deepest thoughts to the 'friend', with results that later often caused her bitterly to rue the confidence she had placed in her.

To the outside world Pip was, by her third term at 'Oaklands', a wicked, dare-devil, casual sort of person, who painted weird distorted figures and buildings, was quite clever at most things except maths, and 'didn't care a damn for anybody'. It was many terms before Tessa learnt that beneath her usually light-hearted and almost blasé exterior, Pip concealed feelings of so acute a nature that the slightest rub could make them hurt badly.

There is supposed to be a 'Difficult Age' during Youth. Its difficult nature is to be accounted for by the fact that it is supposed to be a transitory age, usually ranging between the years of thirteen and sixteen, when one is neither 'flesh, fish nor fowl'. With some the 'Difficult Age' comes earlier in life, and with some later. Pip used afterwards to complain that her's lasted from when she was twelve until she was seventeen, as it was not until she arrived at the latter age that she received her last real 'row' — excluding later ones from police constables for ignoring traffic lights. Whether there really is a 'Difficult Age' or whether it merely forms a suitable subject for preachers at young people's services is a matter of opinion. Some people appear to glide quite securely from childhood to maturity while others of tougher nature have rougher passages interspersed with storms, many of which are weathered in head-mistresses' studies.

There is undoubtedly an inquisitive and 'dirty minded' age, through which school children pass when they are about twelve to fourteen years of age. At this stage they poke around in dictionaries and biological text books in search of sexual details witheld from them by their over-scrupulous mothers. They spend much of their free time sniggering over many reproductions of Renaissance art placed in the library for educational purposes. They enlarge as much as possible that side of their vocabulary which is not to be employed in the hearing of staff or parents. They giggle when they see the school boot boy, import cheap love stories into the school through the agency of day-girls, carry on surreptitious conversations on biological topics, and tell unseemly stories in the shades of the night.

A by-product of sexual curiosity at 'Oaklands' was another system, not so very different from that of friendship, namely the system of 'pashes'. It was the expected thing, among Pip's friends, to 'have a pash' on someone, be she mistress or girl. Those who did not really feel amorously inclined towards anybody manufactured a 'pash' so as not to be out of fashion. From time to time you were expected to change the object of your devotion for the sake of variety. The chief use of the 'pash' system at 'Oaklands' was the scope it gave for artistic talent (many were the red lurid arrow-pierced hearts that were designed), and poetic genius (many girls first discovered a capacity for writing verse in trying to compose love sonnets). The 'pash' system also afforded an excellent and unceasing subject for conversation, mirth and raillery, and added spice to many a wet Sunday afternoon by making that game known as 'Truth and Dare' worth playing.

Many girls had quite genuine 'pashes' on members of staff, or on girls, whose names were ruthlessly wrung from them by the others. These unfortunates suffered and blushed endlessly, having tender feelings paraded before public mockery, and constantly hearing their names coupled teasingly with those of their beloveds.

By way of adding comic relief to this undesirable system, Pip, quite suddenly and evidently without any precedent, fell head over heels in love with Miss Bates. She placed bunches of flowers and tender little poems on her desk, and, amid the laughter of the form and the troubled confusion of Miss Bates, sighed in amorous ecstacy throughout Latin lessons.

Pip's mother was old fashioned. When one day Pip said to her: 'Could you have babies without being married? — I mean what exactly did Daddy do about it?' she replied evasively that Pip did not need to 'know all about that just yet'. Whether there were any necessity for her knowing or not made very little difference as far as Pip was concerned. Having perused biological text books and conversed with her better informed friends, Pip, by three weeks after the beginning of the summer term, knew all there was to be known about sexual relations, and the moral degeneracy of mankind as a whole. She had also made various additions to the side of her vocabulary which, until then, had consisted of two words picked up from her brothers, namely 'blast' and 'damn'.

Pip found her newly discovered knowledge of great interest. One night, as she lay in bed, she began wondering what being 'in love' was really like. Suddenly she realised that, of all people, Tessa Trelawny was the most desirable individual with whom to be 'in love'. From that night on she had a 'pash' on Tessa — at least that was how she described her feelings to herself, although actually, as 'pashes' at 'Oaklands' went, it was something different and much deeper. Tessa Trelawny was all that Pip admired, and, as time went on, she seemed to become steadily more and more wonderful. She was slim — Pip was square and stocky — with sleek brown hair down to her shoulders. She was athletic, won races on Sports Day and carried off swimming and tennis cups. She was quite clever on the rare occasions when she bothered to work hard. She could sing quite well, play the violin, and was a brilliant pianist. (Often Pip watched jealously from afar as she played the piano accompanied by the not so brilliant singing of Chris). She had an attractive face, with a rather turned up nose and a humorous slightly teasing smile. Her clothes always fitted her like a glove, and she had a rather deep and, as Pip put it, 'cultured' voice. She had had various set-backs in her schooling, and so, although fourteen, she was only in Pip's form, of which she was the oldest member.

Perhaps the quality that most made Tessa seem so attractive to Pip was her elusiveness and complete detachment from life that sometimes amounted to vagueness. She seemed to be a person apart, and sometimes Pip would see her seated gazing dreamily ahead of her into an unknown realm where no others, perhaps not even Chris, could follow her. What did she dream about? music? games? people? things? places? Pip did not know. Yet Tessa knew an awful lot about everything that she, Pip, knew nothing about — things like dancing, great musical composers, film stars, and, on occasions, even geometry. Although Chris was her friend, they did not seem very alike, nor inseparably 'thick as thieves' as other friends were. Everybody liked Tessa. She was good at things, and when she came down to earth was amusing, even a leader. She was not a 'goody-goody'.

Pip did not tell anyone what she felt about Tessa for a long time. Finally, many terms later, she told a friend and confident of the moment during that period known as 'after lights', theoretically dedicated to the 'knitting up' of sundry types of 'ravelled sleeves', and too often, in practice, spent in later regretted heart out-pourings. It leaked out to a few people, despite all vows of secrecy, but for some reason it was never widely known, nor was Pip openly teased. When opportunity offered, which was none too often, Pip could chat and laugh with Tessa as though she were just anyone. She liked watching her, and did so surreptitiously as often as possible. Although she was far too reserved to try to force her society upon her, she sometimes wondered whether Tessa knew at all what she felt about her. But she was usually so remote and detached, at least she seemed so to Pip, that she apparently did not take in or bother much about the things that went on around her; so the reason why every term without fail Pip, often in vain, tried to 'bag' a desk immediately behind or in front of her's — a place beside her was too much even to contemplate — never occurred to Tessa.

Whatever she may have seemed to Pip, who, in her thwarted desire for friendship, probably herself painted much of the dazzling cloud of remoteness around her that she often imagined to be present, Tessa actually was no goddess. Seated in the home-bound train that bore her for ever from the precincts of 'Oaklands', one of the events of her career there that particularly stuck out in Pip's memory was a nocturnal escapade she had had with Tessa, which clearly showed that there were occasions when the latter could be quite earth-bound — if not school-rule-bound — when she chose to be.

At about half-term, before Tessa had become irretrievably enmeshed in her friendship with Chris, and before she had completely forgotten the Sunday afternoons she had spent in Pip's company at the beginning of term, the latter came into the grip of one of her rash and dare-devil spasms.

Although the air was sultry, the sun devitalising, and an average of six wasp's carcasses had to be disposed of per meal-time, Matron's edict sanctioning immersion in the waters of that enlarged duck-pond of rectangular shape, politely termed the Swimming Pool, had not gone forth. It undoubtedly was, as Bob bluntly put it one Sunday evening, a 'ruddy swiz'.

'Anyhow why blasted well shouldn't we?' thought Pip, and then was suddenly overcome by the spasm. 'Anyone feel like coming for a swim with me at midnight?' she enquired. A storm of conversation broke forth. Someone betted her a shilling that she would not; someone else said that Parky would probably hear the splashing, and Kitty Smale helpfully wondered what would happen if she were caught. Nobody, not even Bob, seemed anxious to accompany her.

Suddenly Tessa, one of Chopin's studies in her hand, glided abstractedly into the form-room. On being told of Pip's notion she casually remarked that she too considered the temperature to be high, and a bathe at any hour to be highly desirable.

Taking the situation entirely into her own hands, she told Pip that they would set out during the small hours of the next morning, when nobody could fail to be anywhere but in bed...

That night Pip went to bed feeling more excited than she had been for a long time, — not just because of the enterprise ahead, but chiefly because of the company in which she was to undertake it. Tessa, professing to be an adept at waking herself at any hour, promised to come and arouse Pip at about 2 a.m. It seemed hours to Pip before she managed to fall asleep, and when she did she had fitful dreams. First Tessa and she were swimming side by side across the Lake, then a whole flock of swans flew at them flapping their wings. Pip awoke in terror, and then dreamt she was at home and Aunt Mary was giving a Christmas party in the summer, only it was a picnic, and the dog ate up all the plum pudding... Something woke her up. Someone was standing over her with a torch...a burglar...suddenly she remembered — Tessa and the swim in the Lake, of course...

Every floorboard seemed to creak twice as loudly as it ever did in the day-time — particularly just outside Miss Parker's bedrom. The noise they made in opening the Upper IVth window, in order to pass through it into the garden, seemed to Pip to be loud enough to wake everyone in the entire building. Once through the window Tessa ran lightly across the garden, away from the school, down to the drive leading to the Lake. After looking up once at the black windows staring blindly down at her, and wondering for a brief moment whether at any second a horrible horde of spectral and fantastic Matrons and Miss Parkers might not appear gazing through them at her, Pip sprinted over the lawns after Tessa.

Arrived on the drive, Pip was sharply reminded by the gravel that she had brought no footgear of any description with her. Tessa had, and Tessa, although of slender build, was quite muscular and athletic, and an inch or two taller than Pip. After saying: 'Silly little ass', and remarking that she 'would go and forget something', Tessa was magnanimous enough to carry Pip pick-a-back for some fifty yards. Pip's figure was sadly lacking in that slenderness which is attributable to 'airy-fairy' children. She was decidedly tubby, and, after fifty yards or so of sustained agony, Tessa gave up the unequal struggle, and delivered Pip over to further pointed reminders of her folly and forgetfulness from the sharp gravel. Thinking about the event later, Pip was not certain what Tessa and she talked about that night — nothing of great moment anyway...

She was aware rather of Tessa's close proximity than of her conversation, of the slenderness of her waist, the slight rustle of her Japanese dressing-gown as she moved, and of some fragrant scent (actually caused by the Devon Violet talcum powder she had showered upon her body the preceding evening) that she noticed when she walked close to her. Her feet became icy cold and then numb. She forgot that she was walking on a gravel drive. Suddenly an owl swooped by with a piercing ghost-like wail. In surprise Tessa caught hold of her hand for a second, and then with a laugh let it go. Pip wished she had continued to hold it.

Then they reached the Lake, which shimmered in the cold grey light cast by the lightening sky. They both admitted their desire for a bathe was not quite what it had been the previous evening, but they agreed that, for the sake of their reputations, it was vital to dip their shivering bodies in the icy water. Suddenly they realised that they had not brought bathing towels with them.

'We'll have to bathe in the nude and dry ourselves somehow', was Pip's verdict, which they did their best to carry out. Tessa took off her dressing-gown and silk pyjamas. Her slim body stood erect and pure against the dark background. Pip suddenly wanted to put her arms around her neck, tell her how she adored her, and beg her to be her friend again. Instead she took off her own clothes, and they both crept gingerly into the water, the squelchy mud oozing between their frozen toes. Standing thigh-deep in the water, the words of that hymn, in which 'trembling mortals' are depicted as 'starting and shrinking' to cross a certain 'narrow sea' recurred forcibly to Pip's mind. She flung herself into the repelling water, gasping with the shock, and, after swimming frenziedly round in small circles for the space of two minutes, she splashed out of the Lake and found that 'somehow' was a highly unsatisfactory way of drying herself, which left her dressing-gown uncomfortably damp afterwards. Tessa also dried 'somehow', but for some unfathomable reason did not seem to make either her dressing-gown or pyjamas damp.

The sky was brightening rapidly, and Tessa said they had probably set off later than they had imagined. The walked back briskly, not talking much until they came to the place where they had to quit the drive and cut across the garden to the Upper IVth window...

Miss Hannay, the under-matron, always got up early as there were 'so many things to be done'... Hence Pip, peering round the corner, saw that Tessa and Miss Hannay had had an untimely encounter. It struck her that the conversation was rather one-sided, as it consisted solely of challenging questions from Miss Hannay as to how, wherefore, and why Tessa was wandering around the building at that unearthly hour. Tessa, staring straight before her and walking on, made no reply. Suddenly Pip realised that she was pretending to sleep walk, and, thinking Miss Hannay had seen her, decided that the only thing to do was to 'sleep-walk' also. She found it a novel and rather exhilerating experience to have all sorts of questions shot at her by a member of the staff, and to walk on unheedingly.

It was only later, when she was back in bed again, that Pip realised that the coincidence of two girls appearing sleep-walking simultaneously in the early hours of a summer's morning was too extraordinary to be credible to the most ingenuous of people, and Miss Hannay, as Pip knew from bitter experience, was not one of the trustful and believing women of this world. She lay in bed until the bell rang, tortured by mental visions of herself being packed off home in disgrace on the first available train.

As a matter of fact she and Tessa got off very lightly... Afterwards Pip remembered the affair, not so much as a thrilling adventure, nor as an all-but cause of some drastic punishment, nor even as an undertaking that won widespread admiration, but as the closing episode of her brief and already finished friendship with Tessa.

* * *

After I went to Cheltenham in the autumn of 1944 when I was fourteen (the College Principal having decided to take me on as a kind of challenge despite, or because of, my expulsion from Stover, about which my parents confessed), I ceased rigorously to record each separate day in my diary, as I had hitherto. My first day at 'Coll' turns into an account of my first two terms plus the holidays. 'As for "pashes",' I wrote... 'I cannot say I feel violently passionate towards anyone now, which on the whole is a great blessing although just sometimes life feels a little devoid of interest now that the large place Biddy occupied in my thoughts is vacent. Actually I still have sentimental thoughts about Biddy from time to time...' I then proceeed to describe the one or two slight 'pashes' I did, more or less simultaneously, have, and their subjects.

My first reference to Phyll once I was at Cheltenham was in connection with the end of my second term, by which time I had evidently noticed and got interested in her. However, this did not prevent me from being exceedingly taken with E (Keith's early 'girlfriend') when she cropped up in my life during the Easter holidays just before the end of World War II. My encounter with her was, in fact, despite its brevity, closer and more satisfying in many ways than any other 'pash' I had during my schooldays. My diary description of her is as follows:

E. is terribly attractive — slim, brown eyes, curly brown hair & very pretty face — I really cannot think anyone could look & seem much more attractive... Apparently she is supposed to seem old for her age but I do not think she does particularly — anyway I seemed to get on well enough with her & found she was the sort of person one can tell anything to. When she first arrived E. did not take much notice of me — quite naturally as she had plenty to say about what she herself had been doing — but later we became good friends.

Further on I wrote:

E. I think likes me & thinks me quite old for my age. She said she did not feel much gap between us although she was 19. A. [one of E's sisters] said she thought my voice & writing were like E's, which pleased me as there is nobody I should more like to resemble than her...

I was in luck during my stay with the Fs (E's family). The unexpectedly late arrival of an elderly male visitor, which meant he had to stay the night, 'necessitated [as I put it in my diary] E. & I sharing the double bed in my room. Of course I had grown rather keen on E. & the thought of sleeping by her filled me with pleasure.

'Once we had actually settled down it was not very comfortable as I felt I must not move & being excited I spent rather a wakeful night. But lying by E. talking about all kinds of things was wonderful. She said she liked having me there, & I think meant it, & that she was sorry she had no time to liven things up for me much. We cuddled quite close some of the time. I forget whether she put her arms round me at all or whether I did round her, — we certainly said nothing emotional, — but she held my hand a bit.'

On other nights I was less lucky: 'I had dwelt on the fact of my coldness the preceeding night hoping E. would offer to sleep in the double bed with me again & thus act as a radiator. — I was only given an extra blanket.' And on my last night at the Fs 'I washed while E. bathed & told me exactly what her history essay was going to be about. She invited me to come & chat with her in her bed, but Mrs F. said I must go straight to my bed, & so in the end I decided on a compromise by standing in E's room talking & getting cold.'

But when she saw me off on the train back to school a couple of days later: 'To my immense surprise & pleasure she kissed me goodbye & after her waving hand was out of sight I returned to my compartment not feeling far off tears.' Disappointingly, however, she did not answer the long letter I subsequently wrote to her from school, and it was several years before I saw her again, by which time I had left school and grown up.

The fact that E was, or had been, Keith's girlfriend must have been rather confusing — just as when I developed something of a crush on Peter's first girlfriend — at the same time as being in love with Biddy.

I continued to have 'pashes' throughout my schooldays. Towards the end of my time at Cheltenham, as well as feeling erotic about my current closest friend I felt like this about a girl who was actually a trifle younger than I — although she didn't seem it. But the two girls about whom I felt most deeply, these feelings lasting for several years, were Biddy and Phyll.

13

If I was unfortunate over Best Friends and 'pashes' during my schooldays I was lucky over Peter, who was not, as Keith was, away in the army until I was at Cheltenham, and then was too young ever to see any actual fighting. When I was an adolescent we spent quite a lot of time together during school holidays, eventually becoming close friends. We quite often went for cycle rides together. My diary account of one of them illustrates both my companionship with Peter and other aspects of my life as a teenager:

Jan: 6th: Thurs... Peter and I bicycled up to Holne for an art exhibition, to which we had been asked to contribute. I contributed my picture of Holne Vicarage, my sketch from Bishop's Walk & my pencil profile of Daddy's face. The former & latter were recognised & approved of. En route we had the wind with us till Newton & against us to Ashburton. In Newton I bought canvas & white paint. At 'Halfway House', between Newton & Ashburton, I drank some orangeade. At Ashburton Peter developed a puncture (before arriving there we passed a string of about 50 Yank lorries from which some of the occupants hailed us). We had lunch up a muddy lane, Peter furious because of puncture, myself furious because of loss of hair band, & both furious because of poor conditions for picnic lunch eating i.e. muddy lane between high thorny hedgerows. After eating Peter, with my aid, mended puncture & borrowed a pump from a cottage. I, with Peter's aid, tied my hair with string (later Mrs G. gave me a band.) We arrived at Holne at about 2. Mrs G. seemed as if she was mildly annoyed, within herself, because of our late arrival causing her to have to keep lunch hot. Peter & I lunched, others had gone. We then went to see the exhibition which occured in a corrugated iron erection known as 'The Hut'. It was an arts & crafts exhebition & by no means solely a Holne one [Holne is a Dartmoor village] as exhibits came from Nottingham & even as far removed a district as China — in the shape of carved ivory balls & the like. Saw a few people that I knew. Had some brief speech with Miss Cook Hurl. Peter was called a 'supercilious young fellow' by one Miss Bone (Miss Goodison on an intenser & busybodier scale) because he did not approve of the grotesque painty messes from Dartington Hall. We stayed for ages at the exhebition, & had a minor tea there. Pamela [Peter's first girlfriend, aged fifteen, on whom I too had developed a slight crush, I being thirteen] clad in brown costume & stockings, Peter [her brother] in longs — very Sunday go to meeting. Peter (my brother) Pam & myself went for a walk, a circuit over the borders of the moorland. We were all quite foolish. My slight passion for Pam quite dissipated. Think she is rather foolish. Even Peter was not overexcited & only said afterwards she had looked 'rather sweet'. En route for home it became dark, but we were lampless, though only about two people reminded us of this fact. It was quite easy going & we did not byke alongside each other much. We walked through Newton — I would not have had I been alone. We payed due respects to the chip barrow & fish & chip shop before quitting the town.

14

Painting was something that brought Peter and me together. He was very talented (later being offered a place at the Slade School of Art) and drew and painted for hours on end, both while at school and during the holidays. I would watch him painting and comment on his pictures — which he seemed to appreciate. Sometimes we went out sketching together.

I myself often got rather bored during school holidays (especially when Keith and Peter were away) as, when I was at boarding school, most of my particular friends did not live in Torquay. Luckily there was painting: I whiled away hours at home drawing and painting (in oils and water colours). This loomed large during term time also, as many of my diary entries indicate. 'Art,' they say, 'runs in the family.' Keith painted too, so did my mother and relatives on both sides of the family.

The first work I ever sold (at a church bazaar) was a pencil copy of the Yangtse Kiang done when I was eleven. The first original picture I sold was a small oil painting of a Dartmoor waterfall, done on a summer holiday when I was fourteen. It went for three-and-six from a Torquay sweet shop, which had previously sold a copy in oils I did (aged twelve) of a woodland snow scene. As I put it in my diary at about the time the latter picture was sold: 'I thought it might be fun, besides being possibly a paying concern, to try & sell some pictures, & accordingly I carted sundry works of art to all likely, & several unlikely, shops in the town...in the end a little sweet & knick-knack shop opposite the church put 3 pictures in their window. So far one has sold for the vast sum of 2/-...'

I also occasionally sold pictures to fellow pupils, particularly towards the end of my schooldays. I was glad of the cash. Neither my brothers nor I got much pocket-money, and I used sometimes to supplement mine by selling my unwanted possessions at the local pawnshop.

My first portrait was a drawing of my grandmother, done when I was eight. I did childish coloured drawings when I was little and made Christmas cards, some of which got sold at church bazaars, but it was not until I was in my teens that art played a particularly large part in my life. I copied my brothers and started doing oil paintings in the school holidays (copies of other people's pictures) when I was eleven, and received my first school prize for a couple of these (entered for a holiday competition). From then on I spent a great deal of time drawing and painting — which probably helped to keep me out of even more trouble at school than I got into anyway. In my later schooldays I compiled quite a rogues' gallery of pencil sketches and cartoons of my fellow pupils and teachers — mostly done during lessons.

My diary entries give a fair impression of just how large a part art played in my life when I was an adolescent, and indicate both my own and others' impressions of my ability. I still have many of the works referred to in the diary:

Jan: 2nd. Sun:[1944 — I was thirteen] I retired upstairs & copied a photo of Mummy in pencil, which rendered her ugly & unrecognisable, which I tore up, & then a pencil portrait of myself from a mirror; — recognisable, but that is about all to be said for it.

Jan: 7th. Fri: Did oil painting from imagination, & memory of Kent's Cavern, of a cave, containing stalagtites & 'mites &

a sort of little grotto of 'tites & 'mites. The rock was all pink, greenish higher up, with deep red shadows, and Peter said it was a 'Fleshly cave.'

Jan: 18th Tues: Spent a good deal of time doing drawing prep of 'The Enchanted Isle'. It turned out as a crudely coloured poster of palm trees, seashore & various strange creatures including a multi-coloured snail, & a furry man sprouting reindeer horns. It was generally approved. People said it was clever. Booker even insisted it was 'beautiful'.

Sat: April 22nd. I began a sketch of Miss Chamberlain's house from my balcony, following the example of Peter who had just done an overwhelmingly good picture from his bedroom window — I am becoming jealous of Peter in matters pertaining to art, & am horrid enough to almost want his pictures to turn out badly, whereas formerly I wanted them always to turn out well. I sketched again after lunch.

Sunday, April 23rd: I sketched at intervals of the day, having a scene with Mummy because I wanted to miss lunch in order to get the right shadows for my picture, but Mummy forbade me on the grounds that such an action would be uncivilised.[1]

Monday: April 24th. I finished the letter to Keith & embarked on an oil painting of sea, waves, cliffs, a sailor etc from my imagination. It kept me engrossed nearly all day, & when finally finished Mummy & Peter condescended to say it was quite good & clever, although they did not like it.

Thursday: May 18th. In drawing I showed 'Iggly' my sketch of the school which she approved of. I finished my shading model, left over from the previous week, but which 'Iggly' said was too patterny — adding that my works of art as a whole proved that I see things in patterns.

Sun: May 21st. ...I then began painting a copy of my water

---

[1] Getting into trouble over anything to do with painting was very rare. On this occasion I felt decidedly resentful: as my mother painted too she should have known about the importance of painting shadows correctly, even at the expense of lunch-time punctuality.

colour of the school — drawn during one of Friday's lessons — for Miss D. It turned out well when finished, & I think all approved. While I did it people stood over me & watched, oil painting being a novelty for Stover. Carter, Connell & Mary D all asked me to paint pictures for them... Biddy remarked that she had asked Babs to do a sketch of the school for her. I wondered if this was meant as a barbed remark for my benefit, although not said in a meaning tone, as Babs never hardly sketches & does not profess to be any good at, or even to enjoy it, whereas Biddy praised my sketch as much as anyone.

Mon: May 22nd. We discussed art as applied to Stover. Ann said she thought my paintings were crude as a rule. Babs said disapprovingly that I always painted separate leaves on my trees, whereas Pam & other people always did a green haze. We discussed together whether people painted faces like themselves, & decided that some did. We discussed different people's faces & paintings. We wondered whether different people see things differently as often their paintings seem so contrasting...

Wed: May 24th. After I suddenly saw a photo in a magasine of Meg's of an old farmer of 93 — the oldest working farmer in the country — Miss Mitchell thought the face looked like Bernard Shaw's, but that is as may be. I was struck by the photo & thought it looked a fine old face, therefore I promptly settled down to do a pencil copy of it... The copy turned out well for me. It was about the best face I have done so far...

Thurs: May 25th. [Miss Igglesdon] read out the results for the children's wartime drawing competition. Nobody had a prize or medal, but everyone had 1st, 2nd or 3rd class 'highly commended' for their productions. My 2 black & whites which had been sent up gained me 2 1st class commendations. Unfortunately all one gets to show for this is a little ticket on the sheet saying so.

Tues: July 25th. In the evening I copied a photo of Mr Mackenzie King, Prime Minister of Canada. It did not turn out badly, but there were one or 2 mistakes so that my copy was not quite like the photo.

Wednesday: July 26th... I also did a copy of the photo of Curtin, the Prime Minister of Australia. It is about the most successful copy of a face I have yet done...

[*First two terms at Cheltenham plus holidays diary entry – Autumn Term*]: I did a certain amount of painting. I won a prize for a picture containing rather solid looking ghosts. I painted 2 pictures which girls bought for 2/6d. I copied the photo of a film star & did a drawing for the house mag. Mrs Davis [Cheltenham art teacher] thought it a pity that I was not taking up art. Unfortunately I am afraid I have incurred rather a reputation among some people for boastfulness about painting — I am not sure why; perhaps because I do not say pictures I have done are 'simply awful' when people are viewing them & I do not think they are awful, perhaps because I often cart pictures to & from Coll', flapping around if in pencil to prevent smudging... When I went to Prune's in the Easter hols Sybil informed me that 'Iggledy' had said I had a 'streak of artistic genius' (a cheering remark).

The Rest of Term [summer 1945]: I won 1st prize for the holiday art competition on the strength of my painting of a street, which was conspicuously labelled 'oil painting', as though it were some great achievement to have done an oil painting instead of a water color. All the contributions to the competition were displayed in the Milky Way [one of Cheltenham's main, marble-floored corridors].

The rest of the hols at East Portlemouth: I did some more painting...a fairly unsuccessful oil portrait of Nanny almost full face, an oil portrait of Daddy side face which I finished later in the hols & which was quite successful, & a study in oils of flowers in a silver vase — the vase I thought was infinitely more attractive than the flowers... I did portraits of Mummy & Gran & at the end of the hols took (quite well) to clay modelling. I modelled the clay [collected by hand from local clay pits], painted on oil colour, & then varnished the models. I did some animals for the sale, & a drunken sailor & a naked lady for myself.[2]

Christmas Hols 1946: Spent much time playing ping-pong & doing an oil painting entitled 'Wet Lamplight' which I have asked Mummy to send up to the Royal Academy together with one other painting on the offchance that the critics fall under the dillusion that they are masterpieces.

* * *

The Royal Academy did not accept the paintings, and I never again submitted any to it, although as an adult I have had pictures in a number of other exhibitions. On one of the quite frequent occasions when I called on Miss Igglesden during the holidays (she lived in Torquay) she told me that even though I was not taking up painting I would always find some time in my life for it. I suppose she was right: I always have.

[2] This project was not a signal success: the sailor was drunk simply because I did not have the expertise to bake him properly and keep him rigid, and many of the animals (copied from my ornaments), not having been fired properly, did not withstand the vigorous stamping on of prices when being prepared for the church bazaar.

Imaginary Seascape with Sailor (oil; age fourteen)

Stover (watercolour; age fourteen)

15

Art may have 'run in the family', but music did not particularly — indeed my mother seemed rather surprised when, as I grew older, I developed some appreciation of and ability for it. Miss Dence, who as well as being somewhat artistic was exceedingly musical, decided that because I was so badly behaved it followed that I must be bad at music. She was in fact quite surprised to discover towards the end of my Stover days that I was at all good at painting. She remained convinced throughout that I had no musical sense at all and could not even sing in tune — which both my fellow pupils and I considered quite untrue and unfair.

Music, however, was never the pleasure and solace to me that art was, and my musical career as a child was somewhat chequered.

My first piano teacher was my mother. She was not a good teacher and my progress was slow. At Stover, like many of the other girls, I took piano lessons as an 'extra'. I did not do very well at them and my diary records considerable (although only partially justified) teasing, by Biddy in particular, over my performance. My relative ineptitude was not because I was unmusical but because of poor brain/finger coordination (I have never been a very good typist either). Like the others I did one or two of the standard external piano examinations, which I managed to pass, but clearly from my diary I wanted to give up the piano. In January 1944, when I was thirteen, I wrote:

I asked if I need take music during the coming term. Mummy moaned because she said I never did anything I did not like & that it would be useful sometime. She did not commit herself either way. I argued (we both waxed rather cross) that as I was slow at learning & not good generally at playing, in all probability I never should be; also that it was S.C. year & I did not want my short free time occupied by what I did not enjoy doing, & in all probability there would not be a very good teacher again, therefore take it all round it would probably be unprofitable & uneconomical for me to take it. I asked Daddy if I need, but he said he left the matter in Mummy's hands.

Not until I went to Cheltenham was I allowed to give up the piano. A friend of my mother's who taught music there and paid us a visit before I went to the school kindly said that my mouth looked as though it should blow something. Accordingly, when I went to Cheltenham I took up the French horn — about which I previously knew nothing whatever. The instrument belonged to the school, and Keith (by then in the army) paid for my lessons, my teacher being the bandmaster at Cheltenham Boys' College.

When I was at Cheltenham I went to concerts (we were allowed to go to these and very occasionally to the theatre but *never* to the cinema) and found I enjoyed them. I joined the school orchestra, choir and choral class, taking part in school concerts. I acquired some fame as the College French horn player — although people did not always appreciate it when I practised in their vicinity. And it caused some amusement when, taking part in some concert in the Ladies' College orchestra (of which I comprised the entire brass wind section), seated in my shapeless, Sunday, green 'silk' (rayon) uniform dress, I would proceed to tip the accumulated spittle out of my horn's mouthpiece onto the polished Princess Hall floor.

A chapter in *Those Happiest Days*, as well as diary extracts, gives some idea about my musical troubles, ability and early schooldays' career. Like other chapters in the novel, this one conveys some essential truths about me and music at Stover, although the actual story told is untrue: it was based only partly on the event described in the following diary item. The juxtaposition of the novel's chapter with the corresponding diary extract indicates to what extent *Those Happiest Days* was fiction rather than sheer autobiography yet at the same time quite largely mirrored aspects of my own schooldays, some chapters being much more directly autobiographical than others.

' "If Music be the Food of Love, Play On" — But Not If It Be Chopsticks'
(a chapter from *Those Happiest Days*)

Pip was not totally devoid of musical talent. She could sing in tune provided she transposed her notes down an octave to avoid flatness whenever they rose higher in the scale than E. She could usually tell when someone was practising their piece especially badly, and she even derived tolerable enjoyment from listening to music, provided that there was no compulsion to remain awake. For all this the word 'music' for many years conjured up all sorts of nightmarish pictures for her. Pictures of fierce music mistresses waiting to pounce upon her if her fingers wandered ever so slightly from the notes printed, or of gathered audiences smiling derisively while, under compulsion, she sat miserably murdering some string of notes entitled 'Jack Tar', or, later, a simplified version of Handel's 'Largo'...

At the end of every summer term all the girls who learnt the piano had, in turn, to play before the rest of the school and staff. At the end Miss Parker would read out her criticism of each performance. This was always an occasion of misery for

Pip. Her hands trembled and went on to the wrong notes. Often she was obliged to repeat phrases, and, at the end of it all, Miss Parker's openly expressed opinion of her performance was always, to put it mildly, unenthusiastic.

At the close of that summer term when she so distinguished herself in the music exam, Pip was resolved that she would take everyone by surprise and play her piece — the simplified version of Handel's 'Largo' — quite beautifully. They were all doomed to play after supper. Pip practised for a solid hour that evening, despite all complaints from other tremulous musicians desirous of occupying her seat upon the piano stool. She could play it perfectly — at least so she thought. She would darn well make them all sit up. She would play so well that Tessa might stoop to congratulate her afterwards. By the results of her exam she had proved that she could play, so now, this evening, she would just jolly well show them all that she could.

After supper they all gathered in the Hall. Chairs were arranged in rows, and a shimmering haze of staff, their customary ferocity disguised beneath the flowing velvet and silken draperies of evening attire, glided into the seats of honour in the front row. There was whispering, rustling, and the sound of hushed voices, which almost seemed to create the atmosphere of a concert hall. To Pip's tautly strung senses even the mufti dress of the girls, which was worn every evening, assumed a more costly and almost magnificent quality. Chris was in a blue velvet dress, and Tessa was looking charming in a figured silk frock, fitting closely to her figure and leaving bare her white throat. True, Chris had worn the blue velvet every evening for the past week, and Tessa quite often wore her silk dress, yet they seemed to Pip just then to be new, and to have been put on in honour of the evening's events. Bob in a blazer, skirt, and shirt open at the neck, escaped her notice.

To begin with Pip felt confident, and almost looked forward to the moment when she would surprise them all by the brilliancy of her playing. Then she was struck by the formal atmosphere which was created, partly by the way in which the electric lights made the evening dresses of the staff sparkle, partly by the continuous subdued murmur of voices, and partly by the lateness of the hour. A slight uneasiness edged in at the back of her mind. Of course she knew her piece by heart perfectly, and yet... Suddenly she discovered that her hands were becoming hot and a little damp. Breathing a hasty entreaty to Val, her next-door neighbour, to keep her seat for her, she sped from the Hall to the nearest wash-basin, where she ran her hands beneath the cold tap for a few seconds, and then hurried back to the Hall again.

The wraithlike doubt in the deep recesses of Pip's mind began to take form and expand. Just supposing — it was impossible of course — but just supposing she forgot how to play her piece again? Or what if her fingers became so shaky that they fell on to the wrong notes...? And how did that middle bit go exactly...? Did it go up to E flat just there, or only to D? Were all the others whispering and sniggering just to hide their true feelings, or were they really as unafraid as they appeared to be? She whispered and sniggered a bit with Val to try and reassure herself. How about Tessa? Would she play wonderfully? Pip supposed she would. In fact listening to Tessa, and watching her face as she played, became the sole prospect that gave Pip the remotest feeling of pleasant anticipation. Suddenly Miss Parker entered the room, and the performances began.

They went up to play in order of forms, beginning with the juniors, so that Pip's turn was due to come somewhere about the middle; but it was impossible for her to estimate exactly when it would come, as her name would be read out at random from among the others in her form. Pip was amazed and horrified at the alacrity with which everyone seemed to leap up from their seats and advance to the piano. It had been the same at the end of previous summer terms, but this time the feeling of utter self-confidence, apparent in all but herself, struck Pip more forcibly than ever. Small girls of about eight bounced or trotted happily up to the piano when their names were read out, calling out the names and composers of their pieces quite cheerfully, and playing Sailors' Hornpipes and Witches' Dances with far more accuracy and vigour than Pip thought she was likely to display when her turn came. Time went on. Innumerable Hornpipes had been banged out, and it seemed to Pip that it must be drawing near to the turn of her form. Would she be able to cope with all those awful chords? and the pedalling...? She had only recently been instructed in the mysteries of pedalling. Her hands became clammy again. Surely she had not really forgotten how it went? She laid her music book on her knees and tried to finger the piece on it, but her fingers would not function properly without the keys to press down.

It was the turn of her form. Her hands and legs shook, a heaviness in her stomach became apparent, and small drops of perspiration welled through the pores on her nose and upper lip. Would it be she? It was not. It was Val, who, grimacing expressively at her, went up to the piano and rattled something off with more speed than feeling. With sickening dread Pip waited to hear whether her name would be announced next, but it was Tessa who was summoned and who glided gracefully up to the piano with, what seemed to Pip, an almost professional ease. She announced the title and composer of her piece in those low thrilling tones of her's. Pip never heard the words she said — she only heard the voice that uttered them.

Tessa was a real pianist, destined one day to hold audiences spellbound in all the great concert halls of Europe. She held her audience spellbound that night. She had no music before her, but her fingers seemed to be made of some elastic substance, and to know within themselves which notes to race over. A brooch or something sparkled at her throat. Sometimes her hands would wander sadly or caressingly over the keys, while her shining eyes seemed to penetrate the walls of the Hall and gaze out beyond the assembled faces watching her into some far off realm that she alone could enter. Sometimes her fingers tripped merrily, daringly, teasingly over the keys, while her eyes twinkled and a little smile, mocking and challenging, hovered around her mouth. Sometimes with staring eyes she seemed to strike the piano with all her force as though trying to overcome some foe, hidden from all eyes but her's. Perhaps when, after years of training and practising, her technique became polished to effortless perfection, Tessa lost some of her power to imbue her playing with quite the intense feeling which she put into it that night; for as the years passed some of the passion and vitality she once had faded away with the mists of youth.

A burst of applause, louder than any other that evening, followed Tessa's playing. With a feeling almost of nausea Pip heard her name read out. She was to follow Tessa — she, hopelessly bad at music and dithering all over. However well she might play her performance was bound to be the bitterest of anti-climaxes after Tessa. She stumbled forward to the piano, and, in what seemed harsh and unnatural tones, announced that she was about to play Handel's 'Largo'. Her hands were moist and trembling, she was quivering all over, and felt as though her legs would hardly support her. Then she endured one of those terrible moments that sooner or later almost all are bound to go through in some way or another — a moment when all memory deserts one at a crucial moment.

Actors occasionally forget their parts a few minutes before they are supposed to begin performing. Preachers, entering the pulpit without notes, have been known to remember what they were going to say only after an interlude of forced coughing. Seated before the piano Pip discovered that she had not got the slightest notion of how to begin her piece. For a few seconds she sat trying to remember, but failing to do so, and even forgetting that she had the notes she was supposed to play printed in her music book, she thrust her hands on to the keys at random, hoping that instinctively they would hit the right notes. They did not. With her right hand she played two notes a seventh apart, with her left hand two notes a diminished fourth apart. The result was not pleasant to the ear.

Pip grew frantic. There they were all sitting, disgusted, furious, derisive. She simply must do something, play something not matter what it was. She tried to remember how some other pieces went, but she could not. Her mind was a complete blank on the subject of music. She was about to cry out to Miss Parker for mercy when she suddenly remembered that she could play 'Chopsticks'. She'd just got to play something — well if she could remember nothing but 'Chopsticks', 'Chopsticks' she must play. With shaking hands she began, and then suddenly she grew reckless — perhaps she was feeling a little hysterical. She thrust down the loud pedal, and hammered on the notes as loudly as she could. She continued for what seemed to her an indefinite length of time, but which was actually only the few moments needful for Miss Parker's recovery from her shock. Pip was just wondering how and when to end off when Miss Parker's voice rang sharply out saying: 'Philippa, stop this disgraceful performance at once and go straight to bed. I shall deal with you in the morning'.

Life is full of misunderstandings, as Pip learnt to her cost the next day when she completely failed to convince Miss Parker that she had not played 'Chopsticks' out of a spirit of devilry. She was, by that time, so notorious for her obstreperousness, that she failed signally in convincing any of her companions as to the true state of her mind that night.

The playing of 'Chopsticks' at 'Oaklands' was a crime whose penalty was normally the fine of a shilling, which was put into a fund being raised to build a school chapel (a chapel erected on a foundation of fines for leaving books around or not tying socks together before sending them to the laundry). 'Chopsticks' playing was regarded as so grave an offence on the grounds that it 'injured the pianos'. Perhaps it would have been truer to say it injured the all too tunefully tender tympanic membranes of Miss Parker's ears.

Pip had three punishments, two of which were only in theory punishments... The third and only real punishment was inflicted unwittingly by Tessa. As Pip entered the form room on the morning after her vigorous rendering of 'Chopsticks' the matter was being discussed freely by all. She was just in time to hear Tessa say caustically: 'I think the kid's quite daft. I personally don't think that kind of thing is particularly amusing, but I suppose she was just playing to the gallery as usual'. It hurt. It hurt a good deal, and for quite a long time to come Pip kept saying to herself: 'Do I honestly keep playing to the gallery? Surely not, because that time when...'

*   *   *

Corresponding Diary Item:
  Frid: March 24th [1944]. After supper 'Miss Faulder's music pupils' + Maywin, & Pam & Zena to listen, foregathered in the Hall. I felt that if we could just each play in turn with all the others grouped informally around it would be alright. Miss D's ideas unfortunately did not tally with mine. Everybody was seated at just that distance from the piano which would give the air of an expectant audience & thus in all probability cause a trembling or a limp stickiness to the fingers. The piano was turned so that the unfortunate performer's every expression was visible. Miss D & Miss Faulder were seated on 2 chairs in the middle of the Hall, & before the commencement of events, Miss D lectured us earnestly on the solemnity of the occasion. People began playing from the bottom of the school working upwards, & thus I was obliged to sit in wretched apprehension almost until the bitter end. I sat in shaking horror hearing everybody from the 2nd form upwards playing in a remarkably talented sounding way. Eventually my turn arrived, I was summoned forth in spite of my best attempts to hide behind 'Tickles' ' back. My hands, which had gradually grown stickier as my turn advanced, remembered how to begin my piece, although for a few horrible moments before starting my head did not. I forgot almost everything & my piece turned out to sound so horrible as I was feeling — a jangle of discord. My playing was easily the worst. It might have been even more terrible had I known that Ann, Biddy & co. were watching, full of mockery & scorn from up the white

stairs & through the window. I felt dismal in bed at my failure, & also at the fact that Pam had said I had looked cross & fed up while playing when really I was just feeling in a blue funk. It seemed as if my character, without my knowledge & any possibility of preventing it, had appeared on my countenance when I was quite unprepared to mask it, being too taken up with playing wrong chords. It was a little discouraging to be faced by the fact that if my character had appeared on my face at that time, it was a cross & fed up one. Anyhow my face had not belied my feelings as these were just simply terrefied, not angry.

* * *

But things were not always quite so bad, as my diary indicates; and my musical career clearly became very much more successful and enjoyable once I went to Cheltenham. The presence in the orchestra of Phyll (a viola player as well as a pianist) added piquancy to its regular rehearsals — once or twice I used such occasions (not very successfully) to try to get into conversation and strike up a friendship with her.

Just how good a French horn player I really was is debatable. Despite having a reasonably musical ear (essential for this instrument) I was apt to get lost in mid-symphony and was not particularly good at sight reading. However, I twice performed my own compositions quite successfully at internal, informal school concerts — the piano accompaniments having been composed by a music student fellow pupil. They were entitled 'Reveille' (as my diary indicates, this rather unsuitable title was not my choice) and 'Dual Discord' — a title which no one tried to alter. The first piece was rather hymn-like, the second pseudo-Mozartian. And on another occasion I gave quite a competent rendering at an internal Musical Society concert of the fast movement of Mozart's Second Horn Concerto, with piano accompaniment. The following is a diary extract about my later schooldays' musical career:

My First Term at Cheltenham — autumn 1944. I seemed suddenly to turn musical. I took up French horn playing which to begin with I was told was easy as the instrument only boasts 3 valves — which actually is the essence of the difficulties of horn playing. By the end of term, having played in orchestra at the carol concert, I was told the French horn is the most difficult orchestral instrument — the which statement I take with a grain of salt. Everyone praised me about my blowing & the Conductor of orchestra said I ought to make a good French hornist in time.

16

Writing, like painting, seems also to have to some extent 'run in the family' — anyway, it was a pastime of my close relatives. My father was not merely the author of grizzly *Naughtinesses*; as a young man he had written travel articles (he was a great traveller, some of his trips being quite adventurous), many of them getting published, some in the *National Geographical Magazine*. Later he wrote three or four books describing conjuring tricks — his own inventions. My mother was less literary; however she was a regular, newsy correspondent. Keith too was both a punctilious and a graphic, lengthy, letter writer and diarist. Peter, when he grew up, produced humorous verse and turned out to be a good short story writer.

My main writing as a child was, of course, the diary and *Those Happiest Days* (right at the end of the diary I mention starting the latter). However, while these were the major literary endeavours of my schooldays they were not the only ones. I did not go in for writing stories (although at Stover I, and others, used to invent them sometimes and illicitly tell them in bed to the rest of the dormitory after 'lights out'), but I wrote most of the script for a house pantomime at Cheltenham — a skit on aspects of school life — at which I also performed conjuring tricks, taught to me by my father — my first and last performance as a magician. When I was sixteen

I wrote *The Glorious Dead or We the Remembered (a ghostly dialogue),* a short, never performed or published play which throws some light on my response at the time to the prevailing church attitude on the heroism of those killed in battle.

My *Brainfever, or For Those That Sleep in Prep,* performed in the summer of 1947 when I was seventeen at my Cheltenham house Leavers' Party, was a brief comedy whose characters were the mathematical terms, A, B, X and Y, and the Latin prepositions Cum and Dum. As well as being a skit on school work it, like the pantomime script, poked some fun at Cheltenham and its values. Dum, for instance, at one stage says:

'His Subjunctive Highness is an infinitely greater person. He, his father, his grandfather and his great-grandfather have all been Governor Generals of Canada — one of our great families of Empire Builders. While I was having breakfast this morning the postman came with a letter from him saying that Princess Alice [a school 'founder'] had ordered him to see that all the green silks were clean on Speech Day, that the tub was filled up in which they were to wash them, and that I was not to be permitted to rest until this deed had been done.'

The poems which, according to the diary, I began writing when I was fourteen and went to Cheltenham, covered quite a wide range of topics. Sometimes they too were humourous — at the school's or fellow pupils' expense. And as well as love poems to Phyll there were poems about my personal feelings on a variety of matters: poems on religious and political themes and more conventional nature poems, including a couple of poor imitations of Rupert Brook, written when I was fourteen. School work and its tedium was the theme of a sonnet I wrote at seventeen.

To quote from diary extracts written at about that time:

First two terms at Cheltenham, Easter Term. Some doggerel about a new girl's impressions of Coll' by me was put in the very small house mag; — went to make the end of term pleasant.
The Rest of Term [summer 1945]: I distinguished myself in 3

more ways during the 2nd half of the term. Miss Dobbing approved of my French play which she read out with great gusto during a lesson. After exams Mrs Greenlaw set an odd English prep. We had to choose whether to write a mock heroic poem, finish off the story of Beatrix Esmond, insert 3 or more verses into Gray's Elegy or write a conversation in the style of Jane Austin. I chose to do the first, & chose the impending 'St. Hilda's Day' [a major Cheltenham Ladies' College event] as my subject. All the people who read the poem were amused by it & Mrs Greenlaw said she advised me to send it in to the editor of the Coll. Mag. & herself showed it to the St. Hilda's East committee, which, I believe, includes the head of Coll' & 'Popeye' [the College Principal, Miss Popham].

I did twice have poems published in the College Magazine but not the St. Hilda's Day one. As it was mock-heroic, hence poked fun at sacred school matters, the rather circumspect editors (the school librarians) may have deemed it not quite suitable for inclusion.

17

As the diary indicates, games, and sport in general, loomed large at school, and to be good at games was, as at similar boys' schools, exceedingly important. My initial periods of unpopularity and unhappiness at Stover and later Cheltenham were also periods of athletic incompetence. As I became more popular, hence happier, so my athletic prowess increased.

Not that I was ever a great athlete. I managed to get into the Stover 1st and Cheltenham 2nd lacrosse teams (the latter never playing an actual match that term because of bad weather) through the device of being 'goalie'. I was not actually an especially effective goal-keeper, but it was not a hankered-after role and by its means I managed to achieve the coveted team membership. I could run quite fast, but never fast enough to come more than third in Stover Sports Day races.

Various outdoor activities helped to occupy the school holidays, particularly swimming, which I loved. I learnt to swim when I was six — at the same age as I learnt to ride a bicycle and row with one oar (I could manage two by the time I was eight). I could never swim very fast or stylishly, nor did I ever achieve my ambition of Swimming the Channel; however I could, at an early age, swim quite a long way. When I was twelve I swam across Torbay from Torquay harbour to Paignton pier — two to three miles — in a choppy sea in early autumn, accompanied by my bored brothers in a rowing boat. I performed this feat as a sort of bet (not a real one). I was in the sea, unoiled, for about three hours and got very tired, hungry (initially), cold, waterlogged and, ultimately, rather cross — then played table tennis almost as soon as I got home. People were surprised that my mother, so 'stuffy' about many things, allowed me to do anything deemed so dangerously strenuous.

My diary contains two references to this swimming feat. The first: 'The conversation dealt largely with sea-bathing, Mummy recounting how when 10 I was supposed to have been nearly drowned at Croyd, & how I swam from Torquay harbour to Paignton pier when 12. Apparently Mummy thinks that I am not proud of this latter feat. Did she but know it however, it is the incident of my life which, I think, fills my soul with more pride & glory of remembrance than any other.'

The second diary reference to the swim bears out how proud of it I was: 'She does not know that I have sea bathed on frosty Xmas holiday evenings & that when I was 12 I was 3 hours in the sea when swimming from Torquay harbour to Paignton pier, 2 to 3 miles.'

Peter and I did go for a sea bathe one Christmas Day in Torquay. We had eaten too much for dinner and wanted to get up an appetite for Christmas tea. And the diary contains an account of my near-drowning one day in Torquay when it was so rough that bathing was forbidden: I was repeatedly submerged, quite close inshore, by great breakers crashing against the shelving Oddicomb beach.

In the summer I also did some unpolished pony riding on Dartmoor. There was plenty of ping pong (which I was reasonably good at, although I never was at tennis) on a table in the Rectory basement. And all the year round there were the often quite long cycle rides.

The importance of sport at school comes out in particular chapters in my two early novels. The diary also is full of references to games, gym, my ambitions to get into a team and concern lest I did not — as full as it is of references (sometimes pleased, sometimes worried) to school work, exams, revision, Weekly Marks averages and so on. The following two diary extracts illustrate the importance of games to me during my schooldays. The first is a brief account of a Stover netball match when I actually captained the Twelve and Under team. The second is an account of my athletic prowess — and lack of same — during early days at Cheltenham:

Feb: 12th Sat: ...The match was a success. The weather was good & we won by 21-7 goals. I was informed that I played well, & that I did all my captain-stuff well, in talking — I managed to rake up subjects to talk about varying between the game, & the bad fish we had had for lunch the preceding day. After the match we ate, & were even able to go round the terraces & grottoes under my supervision! The Newton Grammar team were all pleasant & talkative, but they all had accents of course, & were very large and sophisticated looking for their ages. It was generally said that it had been a good game, & Miss D even offered congratulations for the way in which we had played, saying that we had worked well together as a team.

[*My First Two Terms at Cheltenham*] During my first term I did quite badly at gym & from my grades, was evidently considered to have a mediocre deportment [good deportment was highly rated at both Stover and Cheltenham, and at the latter was apt to be equated for some reason with good behaviour]. I have Field [games] 3 times a week (at most) & accordingly had little chance in distinguishing myself at hockey... I played goal in the house lax junior in the one match which we lost. I was told I played well 1st half. Actually I was a bit cut up that I was not captain or vice of our team, although my name was put forward, as besides being oldest in the team, all the others, barring the captain a U.C.3, [one of the 'years', or forms, at Cheltenham] were 1.2's & 1.4's. Luckily several nice things happened at the end of term so that I was able to return home with a tolerably satisfied feeling in the pit of my stomach. I got my house junior & am therefore entitled to wear an unobtainable bit of white cloth with C.L.C. & a cross in one corner on my games tunic.

18

Throughout my schooldays perplexing questions about religion and Right and Wrong arose, and my religious views remained somewhat confused. From the age of about twelve, while still believing in God, I began to question the divinity of Christ. Notions of 'dishonour' and 'discipline', all-important terms at school — and at home — were somewhat baffling. For instance, at around twelve I was discovered by my parents reading my father's copy of *Rebecca*. They forbade me to continue on the grounds that it was too morbid (because of the suicide that features in the story) for someone of my age. (Strangely, they did not object to the, by current standards, sexually explicit *Gone With the Wind*, which I was actually allowed to read on a Sunday as it was 'a classic'.) I disobeyed, was caught reading the book again and promptly sent to bed. Back at Stover I found there was a copy in the school library. Naturally I read it. Rather gleefully I told my mother this the following holidays.

'Oh, how could you be so dishonourable, dear,' she responded, more in sorrow than in anger, 'when you knew your father and I didn't want you to?' But I don't think I felt particularly guilty; after all, they had chosen to send me away to boarding school, so why shouldn't they take the consequences?

At Stover we were for ever being 'put on our honour' not to commit some misdeed or another. Eventually this struck me as silly. It might be disobedient to talk in bed 'after lights out' (which nearly all of us invariably did), but why was it 'dishonourable' and not simply common sense to desist if we heard footsteps approaching the dormitory? I said as much to Miss Lydgate once when she was expressing views on the 'dishonourableness' of breaking the no-talking-in-bed rule.

My interest in and concern about religion (Peter and I used to sample different denominations) emerge clearly from my writing at the time. I was much exercised about the whole subject, my doubts and questions prompted partly by the religious tone of the schools I attended, partly by my family background. The following are extracts from my diary on this topic:

Jan: 13th. Thurs: ...I then went up to Gran and argued violently... I admitted I was not a Christian & she told me to pray to be made one. Why should I pray to be made something the doctrine of which I do not believe? She seemed a little too dogmatic about '2nd adventists' theories i.e. the disappearance of Christ's elect before the awful times before the end of the world. (What do all these matters concern us anyhow? They should not make any difference to the sort of lives we live.) She seemed a little too self-satisfied about her own 'tram ticket to salvation'.

Jan: 25th Tues: After lights, I flung wide my window, & leant out into the night. The wind was blowing great guns, & my hair. The trees looked black & mysterious silhouetted against the starless sky. I felt then close to God as I have only felt once before — when I vowed to take no notice of Biddy (a vow I soon broke). I came to a realisation that God is in everything, in order that he can work out His purpose. In the winds, seas, earth, & skies. In the actions of men, in all pain, pestilence, hardship, poverty & suffering. In all life, death, pleasures, joys, sorrows, creations; & in short all in the universe & Heavens, that is dead, alive, spirit, created all vices, instincts

& passions. Somehow when I returned to bed it seemed an anticlimax to hear all these live creatures giving voice to the said mirths & vices, but I felt happy. Leaning out of the window with my hair blown like streamers in the wind, I had felt that God was close beside me, supporting & strengthening me.

Feb: 6th Sun: At church there was a new preacher — goodness knows who — who made an unusual sermon dealing with the fact that the world is good...

'And God saw everything that He had made, & behold it was very good'. I did not agree that the world is good. I think that originally it was, as states the text, but men have made it bad, & it is up to them to put it right again. The preacher however did not point out any such moral. The whole service annoyed me. There seemed no point in gathering around singing, chanting, saying and hearing things which are so oft repeated as to be well nigh meaningless, & which render no spiritual benefit. I am sure God does not want one to spend the sabbath in such a pointless way.

Sun: April 2nd. Three thoughts struck me during one of the sermons, but not I am afraid, as a result therefrom.

(a.) Why did Our Lord contradict Himself by at one time saying 'My yoke is easy, & my burden light' & at another time saying 'Straight is the gait & narrow is the way which leadeth unto life eternal'? thus indicating the easiness & then the difficulty of the good life. I solved this problem myself going home from church. I suppose that in any case a good life is difficult, but under Christ's yoke it is supposed to be easier than to try to lead in one's own strength, or by following another religion.

(b.) My mind reverted to what Miss D. had read the week before from the 'Screwtape letters.' From them it could be gathered that all pleasures were made by God & therefore all were good so long as not carried to excess, or used in the wrong way, therefore all Mummy's theories about never drinking or gambling can be defied. These are pleasures, therefore made by God, therefore not wrong if carried on rightfully & in moderation.

(c.) Another thought that struck me was with regard to a statement made recently by Daddy. He had said that, according to some book, most of the referances in the authorised Bible to 'everlasting' punishment etc; were mistransalations & that the proper wording should be 'Punishment for a time.' I found an arguement that could prove there to be everlasting punishment anyway. In Christ's parable of the unforgiving steward, He closed by saying that the steward was cast into prison until he could pay off all his debt. This would be impossible & therefore the man would always remain a prisoner, thus indicating that there is an everlasting punishment. Mummy pointed out that these parables had only been recited on the spur of the moment, & therefore must not be probed too deeply. I felt inclined to agree on this point as after all if anyone is likely to be punished for ever it is me & therefore I would be glad not to take the parable too literally.

Sun May 28th. We could not go to church & so had choral communion service here, which we were all obliged to go to. To use Daddy's language, the service was 'spikey', & I cannot say that the sight of the comunion sacrament moved me. Of course it was all solemn & reverant, yet the ceremony struck me as seeming rather superficial & almost grotesque, to put it baldly. Somehow to worship, I do not feel that it should be necessary to have to eat & drink. I am sure if I did it, I should be in quite a wrong frame of mind, wondering whether I would gurgle while drinking, or with similar thoughts flitting across my brain, not thinking of God, or what the sacrament stood for at all.

[*My First Two Terms at Cheltenham*] Early in the term I nearly asked if I could go to Glenlee as it was a new house where I thought I might be somebody who 'counted' in a small degree, also because I do not like S.A. [St. Austin's, my first Cheltenham house] & should like to be in a house with Rosabelle Griffiths ('Rags'). I prayed to do the right thing, as I did not know whether to ask to go from S.A. or not, & as immediately after I read bible verses which seemed to tell me to stay at S.A. I did nothing further about going to Glenlee.

April 9th Mon: 1945: ...in the evening Peter & I went to a P.B. [Plymouth Brethren] service at St. Marychurch. It was held in a small mean little hall & the congregation seemed mostly — as I had expected — poor. The adress was intended to set before us the holiness of God. The speaker was emotional, appeared to lack any logical sequence of ideas, possessed a sickly grin, repeated himself innumerable times, & possessed a repetoir of about 6 different gestures which he did in turn.

Mon: April 17th. At supper we talked about religion. I decided that it does not matter whether we believe in Christ but His principals, which I think was what he meant us to do, as by saying 'I am the way' he meant his doctrines were the way. It was the apostles who especially admonished belief in Him. Faith in Jesus helps many, though it is good to support missions.

Monday June 27th–Friday July 21st. In the evening I went to a salvation army meeting... I did not approve of the service as it seemed almost too informal to be sufficiently reverant. There was not kneeling down for prayers, of course, & people wispered & giggled softly during the most solemn parts of the proceedings. At one point in the proceedings a child, who I am sure had whooping cough, was sick just behind me & had to be taken out... Lastly a bonnetted individual gave a long drawn out gospel adress on the theme that class does not alter the soul. In the end the adress was cut up by prayers & 'prayer songs' & many, myself included, went before the end of the service. This part of the service was rather horrible for me as anyone 'unsaved' was asked to step out & I had a horrible feeling that I must — it was a little like the feeling I get on the edges of cliffs, that I must cast myself headlong from it. However I knew that if I once proffessed myself not to be a fully fledged Christian I should never be let out of that place alive as I should have been kept there until Doomesday, or else have made some untrue declaration of faith. I would have required sound logical arguement, not the sentiment & emotion that probably the 'Salvationists' would have put across...

The V.P.S. Camp [a Varsities' and Public Schools' 'camp' — in reality a house-party I went to during the 1945 summer holidays when I was fifteen]. One morning I had coffee with Paddy Mowle, my Junior Officer & a C.L.C. [Cheltenham] girl. We had a long religious discussion on Christianity as a whole which received no satisfactory conclusion. Religion was fairly piled on with a trowel at camp, & before going I had another long & equally unsatisfactory discussion with the comandent of the camp. I wrote a miserable letter home asking whether I could quit camp early & Mummy wrote back saying I could, but they were very cut up when I took them at their word, especially as my journey home was a muddle & I came via London & was not 'seen across'. [My father believed I might be a victim of the White Slave Trade were I not accompanied across London.] If I had known how hurt the 'High Comand' would be at my early quittal of camp [which was supposed to be a 'treat'], I probably would have stuck it out, but in every other way I was glad I came home early. I felt very miserable my first day home & I seemed to have recently heard so often that one could attain happiness by being a Christian, & so, as there seem really to be as many arguments in favour of the soundness of Christian doctrines as against I decided to give it a try. Certainly life seemed to take on a brighter hue afterwards.

I did not stay a 'born again' Christian for long — my parents in fact seemed sceptical that this re-conversion had been genuine, so bad did I remain.

By the end of my schooldays I had become, or more or less become, an agnostic, as my poem 'Plaint' (written when I was seventeen and published in the school magazine) indicates. Miss Popham, a keen high Anglican, tried in vain to persuade me, when I was fifteen, to go to Confirmation Classes. I declined to do so on the grounds that I didn't want to be confirmed and anyway hadn't time to attend the classes as I was in the Gilbert and Sullivan opera chorus. When she pointed out that I might learn something from going to the classes I denied this, saying that, as a parson's daughter, I knew all about the subject anyway. My father was equally unsuccessful when he too, somewhat cautiously, broached the subject.

My one or two teenage religious poems reflected my uncertainty and changing attitude, 'Behold I Stand at the Door & Knock' carrying a thoroughly Christian message, unlike 'Plaint', which ran thus:

Plaint

Are chemicals our only driving force?
Our natures naught but tenuous threads of nerve
And potent fluids from our glands that serve
To lubricate the engine of their laws?
The essence of our natures is it found
In those parental gifts we're forced to take,
So that our personalities are bound
By chains of steel impossible to break?
Does every protoplasmic mass called man
Receive from some all-ruling force behind
An independent motive power that can,
Unhampered, frame the structure of his mind?
Or are man's whims, his follies and his spleens
Caused merely by hereditary genes?

19

Although preoccupied by religious questions during my schooldays, political matters did concern me to some extent too — increasingly as I got older (at Cheltenham I specialised in history). War and peace and general issues loomed larger in my mind than party politics. (My parents seldom discussed or seemed particularly interested in the subject, which was not apt to arise at school either.) However, some thoughts about this do surface in later diary entries made at the time of the post-war 1945 General Election, which happened when I was fifteen.

Not surprisingly, as war was raging at the time, how to prevent another one breaking out cropped up in at least one conversation I had when I was twelve or thirteen. A group of us at Stover discussed this one night as we sat illegally chatting on someone's bed after 'lights out'. The answer, we concluded, was to form a world government.

The dropping of the atom bomb on Hiroshima does not merit a mention in my diary on the day this occurred. Other matters were uppermost in my mind. Not until two or three days after the event is it referred to in the diary. My entry for Friday August 10th 1945 runs thus:

'A card came by morning post headed "The Army August."

It was from Peter of course. He said that owing to the likely rapid termination of hostilities (the first atomic bomb fell on the 7th) he was trying to get out of the army...'

It was, at the time, the ending of the war with Japan that mattered to me rather than how this happened. The day before it ended my parents and I went for a row on the nearby estuary and, when the tide went out, got marooned by mistake for so long that I was dreadfully afraid we would miss the peace announcement and all the attendant fun. My diary contains no comment whatever on the Nagasaki bomb but my entry for the day peace was declared runs thus:

VJ Day Wed. Aug. 15th. One of the village came & told us before breakfast that it was peace so I decked myself out as patriotically as possible with red white & blue in my hair and red & white belts, order of the garter-wise, about me on the blue background of my shirt. Later I donned my blue cardigan, a red white & blue buttonhole, & some lipstick. I set off to sketch in the morning, but as my sticky oil painting kept blowing in my face I finally rode on my byke to Southpool instead. In the afternoon Daddy drove us in the car to Kingsbridge where we saw a 'Marx Brothers' film. When we came back from Kingsbridge we went to church & fed, & then set off again in the car, this time to Plymouth to join in V.J. revelrie. I stood on the running board of the car for quite a long way & got averagely cold. What struck me as we rolled along was the singular unresponsiveness of the country people we passed & hailed & who, in the main, regarded us with looks of fixed scorn. There were great jollifications at Plymouth — dense throngs, hooting ships, bonfires, searchlights, dancing in the streets & fireworks let off from the ships so that the sky was often filled by showers of coloured stars casting shimmering reflections on the shiney rippling, black sea. We picniced on the way home, & I finally fell asleep in the car. We were not home until the early hours of V.J. the 2nd Day.

However, the implications of dropping the atom bomb must fairly soon have been borne in on me, for a few months later, when I was fifteen, I wrote the following gloomy poem:

Peace

What is our peace but battlefields red
That are stained with the blood of thousands dead?

What is our peace but the sorrow & crying
Of those who are starved, or sick & dying?

What is our peace but the anguish sore
Of women whose lovers will wake no more?

What is our peace but the slaughter of those
Who a year or so gone were our deadliest foes?

What is our peace but endless quarrels
On armies & councils, justice & morals?

What is our peace but the growing dread
That in a few years we shall all be dead?

What is our peace? I cannot say more
Than this – it is no less than undeclared war.

And a year or so later, while I was still at Cheltenham, we were set an essay on 'The Pen is Mightier Than the Sword'. The teacher was favourably impressed by my effort. I argued that while this statement might have been true in the past it no longer was in the atomic age.

My short, never performed play, *The Glorious Dead*, written in the autumn of 1946, is quite revealing about some of my teenage attitudes to war:

'The Glorious Dead' or 'We the Remembered'
(a ghostly dialogue)

Scene: The men's quarters in the Purgatory Prison. The Divine Trial of War Martyrs has just concluded. Enter two of the martyr ghosts.

Mike: How did you get on, Snooks?...

Snooks: O well I've got to work on the land down in Hell for a couple of thousand years...

Mike: Tough luck...especially after all that grim business you went through in Normandy. Lay in a ditch slowly bleeding to death for three days didn't you?

Snooks: Yep, but that didn't make much odds with the jury. You see I never wanted to join up. I tried to be a conscientious objector and so get out of it all — even turned Quaker on the strength of it — practically broke Mother's heart, that did — she's a Baptist. It didn't work though. I got all tied up in my arguements and contradicted myself, so they shoved me into Khaki after all.

Mike: Still you were a war martyr in the end. The other day before the trial I got leave of absence for a couple of nights. I went down and paid the family a visit, and heard all the wonderful things they said about me. It was Remembrance Day and Mother began to cry that night. The Governor tried to comfort her by saying that anyhow I was a saint now with a crown and harp and all that because I was a war martyr... They never spotted us in time in our rubber dinghy.

Snooks: The jury didn't care a hoot about all the war martyr racket. Although I bled in a ditch for three days I never loved God with all my heart nor my neighbour as myself, and I always let down Lizzy, my little wife, when Kit was on leave.

Mike: Still I don't call it fair. You died for England and liberty. When I was on my leave of absence I went to church and they all sang about us — the blokes killed in the War. According to them we're all valiant hearts who went through dust of conflict and battle flames and are waiting for the Almighty's trumpet.

Snooks: Don't know so much about trumpets. Personally I'm waiting to hear the Infernal siren hooting out at six every morning for us to start work. Anyhow I didn't die for England or liberty, but only because I couldn't clear out of the Jerry range quick enough. How about you? Did you die for the Empire and freedom and all that?

Mike: O I don't know. I hadn't much choice about joining up of course, but I expect I would have anyhow. Funny thing though, the witnesses didn't say much about the War, nor even about my posthumus V.C... They talked more about the time when I went to read to an invalid aunt instead of going to the pictures with Sammy and Jill. They seemed to harp the whole time on funny things like a bob I gave to Dr Barnardo's once when I was a kid instead of buying a book I wanted...

Snooks: There mate, what did I say? It's all ruddy rot, this business about dead soldiers. 'Age shall not weary them nor the years condemn'. If age don't weary me, ploughing Infernal fields for two thousand years will...

* * *

Here and there in the diary I express a number of political views, many of them related in some way to the War. On Sunday April 30th there is an entry about my reaction to a nearby air raid:

I awoke, feeling hot in bed, at about twenty to 4. Shortly I heard the 'alert' go & thenceforward felt troubled & unable to sleep, as at that critical stage of the war, with an invasion of Europe impending, the country full of Yank troops, & barrage balloons sailing above Torquay, one could not feel comfortably certain of one's safety from the bomb that flyeth by night after a siren had sounded.

I automatically strained my ears for the drone of planes, & for sometime heard nothing. After a while, however, as I lay wearily hoping & praying for the 'all clear' so that I could resume my slumbers in peace, I heared the intermittant rumble of distant planes, & then the low distant thunder of guns. I lay on, feeling frightened, (being safely installed at school for the better part of the year, I had hardly been in any raids, & therefore there was some excuse for my feelings of fright at the prospect of a possible raid.)[1] Suddenly the firing sounded louder & nearer, & fearing that planes might be coming over to bomb Torquay, I rose from my bed & went downstairs along with Mummy, Daddy, Gran & 'Goody' — Peter remained in bed throughout.[2] I sat on the arm of a chair in the study. Later Mummy & Gran went & sat in the shelter, & I looked out of the dining room in the direction of Plymouth, which was suffering the raid. Orange flares stood out like lamps in the sky. Orange darts of fire — shells bursting — leapt about the sky, & the distant beams of searchlight played around. Daddy, Goody & I then wandered around in the road where I felt quite safe as I could easily dive into the shelter if anything happened. We watched what took place

[1] I was in fact terrified of air raids, which I seldom experienced, and longed to escape from where they might possibly happen. I was frightened even when my father, as an Air Raid Warden, received by telephone the pre-alert 'yellow warning' message. On one occasion my mother tried to calm me with the promise of a much longed for new bicycle.

[2] Unlike me, he was not at all frightened, once even watching a 'tip and run' attack on Torquay with interest while I cowered petrified beneath the kitchen table.

over Plymouth, search-lights, flares, firing, sudden brilliant flashes, possibly by H.E. [high explosive] bombs, great flares of light starting up, probably something eg. petrol dump, going up in flames, & the turning light which signaled up to our planes. Every now & then we heard weird & uncanny noises rather like a mixture of a very loud-voiced Fifi crying outside a window & an owl with a sore throat, these strange sounds were the sirens of the ships in the Bay, which had scattered and were signalling to each other. The raid over Plymouth was not very bad & it did not appear that incendiaries were dropped. Probably not more than about 30 enemy raiders went over. After about an hour, by the time I was thoroughly cold & almost dozing leaning against the garden wall, the all clear went, & I returned to bed & to slumber-land...

In June 1945 I expressed views about 'pilotless planes' ['buzz-bombs'] among other things:

Two final facts to remark on: (a.) the weather was continuously glorious at that time. (b.) the political situation, on which I do not ponder deeply as a rule. Slow progress continued in Normandy, & the Germans by way of reprisals & to aid their propeganda, began using pilotless planes, sort of flying bombs, on London & the S. coast — not near Torquay. As these machines cannot survive, because they crash & explode, they seem to me to be a great wast of metal etc. Surely it would be better, except perhaps from propeganda purposes, to carry on as before?

My comment, made at about the same time, on an attempt on Hitler's life was merely that it 'had apparently not caused him harm other than burns & semi de-bagation' and that 'A certain amount of anarchy had broken out in Germany.' A little later I wrote:

...and the news was good, but showed one ghastly photo of prisoners of the Japs, looking like living skeletons, who had been freed in Manilla. As regards the present state of the news — a subject I am always a bit hazy about — the Western lines are within 100 or so miles of Berlin & the Russians have been only about 20 miles away for months. Buzz bombs & V.2's are still banging about I believe & a few planes have been bombing parts of England.

When during the 1945 Easter holidays (just before the war in Europe ended and I was fifteen) I went to stay with the Fs (our family friends in Oxford), I found myself in social situations, when out with E and when at their home, where I was decidedly out of my depth, as the diary indicates. Mrs F was gregarious and encouraged visitors to drop in. My account of one social evening reveals both my social gaucheness and my shame at being so apolitical:

We arrived back to find the house swarming with friends in for coffee. There was an ex-prisoner of war who looked a picture of good health & a Wren friend of A's & a friend of her's who had appeared the preceding day. As was to be expected, the ex-prisoner of war was vague & non-comittal in the extreem concerning his imprisonments & escapes. I sat in a rather isolated spot between the coffee things & Mrs F. whose voice was usually directed elsewhere, & therefore I did not raise my voice much & felt slightly 'left out.' This fact together with the teatime events went to prove that I need much more practice in holding my own at social gatherings where there are none of my family & many of those present are strangers. I was filled with horror when Mrs F. decided to find out everyone's political views & began on me. I shamefacedly had to admit the childishness of not having formed any. Later Mrs F. asked whether my family ever engaged in political discussions & shamefacedly again I had to admit to the contrary. Had I thought I might have said we made up for it in religious discussions & debates.

This social ineptitude may have come as something of a shock to me. I was quite a talkative, gregarious child, accustomed to chatting to members of my father's parish and the quite frequent visitors who came to stay.

By the run-up to the General Election (a month or two after my visit to the Fs) I had evidently become less apolitical — I listened to election speeches on the radio and had views about them, as expressed in the diary:

Thurs. 31st – Tues. June 6th Having heard the electoral speeches of Churchill, Atlee & Lord Samuel (Liberal leader in the House of Lords) I have formed the political views which were so sadly lacking during my sojourn at the Fs'. I did not think much of Churchill's speech. He failed to say deffinately what plans the Conservatives had in mind for reconstruction. He dogmatically condemned Socialism, without, it seems to me, introducing sufficient examples or proofs to back up his arguements. In fact his whole condemnation of the Socialists seemed to me to be made up of sweeping & flowery statements of a highblown literary flavour, & poorly backed by sound reasoning. It almost seemed as though Churchill were striving to condemn the Socialists just because they were in an opposition party & not because he could produce very tangible proof against their beliefs. This is just the impression his speech created on me, but probably my ideas are quite wrong. Having just read a book on Churchill, which left me favourably impressed about him, I was slightly surprised by his speech, & by the fact that I myself would not support his party if I were voting.

From the Liberal & Labour representatives' speeches, it also seems obvious that Churchill has adopted quite contradictory attitudes with regard to having a general election and the time for having it. Mr Samuel did not really define very clearly the Liberal aims which just seemed to consist in projects of future legislation — which anyhow the Conservatives would carry out to a certain extent. The legislation of the past has been carried out mainly by the Liberals but all the same many evils still exist which I think may only be abolished by more state control. Anyhow Britain has not been a Utopia under former Liberal &

Conservative governments & so there is no reason to believe that future ones would make her so. Socialists have never yet been given much chance of trying their hands in British politics & so why not let them try now. After all if it does not succeed in righting many evils, or is inclined to create havoc in some way, such a state of affairs need not continue indeffinately, at the next general election the Liberals or Conservatives can be voted back to office, & any evils created under a Labour government can be rectified. Anyhow I am all for experimenting with new methods — the old ones have not succeeded in very many ways to put a stop to very many evils.

Finally the British people are not revolutionary as a whole & are a little inclined to tread life's paths with a leisurely if measured step, so that even if the Socialists did come into office, ten to one no very drastic or ultra rapid & revolutionary changes would be made. In many cases Socialism in Russia has not succeeded in the object of creating a perfect state. That may be because the Russians tried to revolutionise affairs too sweepingly. The Russian temperament is not like our's, & the more gradual, less revolutionary & more Christian methods a British Socialist government would adopt might ensure success where Russian Socialism has not yet succeeded.

Notwithstanding this diary entry, a few days later I wrote: '...after hearing [on the wireless] the Chancellor of the Exchequer — Sir John Anderson — hold forth (his speech a little shook my socialist views).' I do not spell out why in the diary, but shortly after, 'I heard part of the speech of the Labour minister Alexander, formerly at the Admiralty... As he did not seem to have anything original to say, moreover had rather a common voice I failed to hear his speech through to the end.' The shocking snobbery betrayed by this comment, and others in the diary, was no doubt the fault both of my parents — especially my mother — and of my schools.

My class attitudes as a child may have been appalling, but my attitude towards 'the enemy' was surprisingly tolerant. This may have been partly because I myself did not suffer unduly during the War, none of my relatives being killed or injured, partly because of Biblical 'love thine enemy' precepts. An entry made in the summer of 1945 reveals even a hint of disloyalty towards my own side:

Mr Churn [a Eurasian family friend staying with us] had been, without any even specified reason, imprisoned in a dungeon in Calcutta, was continually told to own up, to, he did not know what, & was not given enough clothes, anything to do anyone to talk to most of the time or any good food. It was interesting to hear for once the experiences of someone imprisoned by the Allies.

As for the Germans, a diary entry for early May 1945 throws light on this:

I had 2 political discussions. One in the study chiefly with Pauline whose father apparently holds the view that, 'the only good German is a dead one,' and one with Jinny who believes that Germany must be sternly repressed after the war, & with whom I argued that too stern & longlasting repression will surely breed hatred & later further wars. Although this latter was rather heated as Jinny — I imagine — & I both felt rather fed up with each other, yet I believe it was a means of raising me in her opinion (& her in mine), as later we had quite an amicable discussion in which she apologised for any heatedness displayed by her, & we mutually agreed that such discussions are a good show.

On VE Day Eve — Monday 7th — I felt revolted by the fact that, as VE Day would give us an extra free afternoon, lots of people hoped it would not be the next day when most U.C. would be having a free afternoon anyhow. Thinking of the lives that would be saved by VE Day coming as soon as possible, I felt shocked by those sentiments & when asked what day I wanted it to be on said, I imagine rather coldly & aloofly, that I hoped it would be the next day. On the news later it was proclaimed that my wish would be granted.

20

Despite successes achieved and enjoying many things during my schooldays, I was not, by and large, a particularly happy child. This may have been because of quarrels with my parents, unfulfilled ambitions, unrequited love and the general trouble I got into, plus the fact that my self-esteem, hence happiness, was evidently dependent to a large extent on others' approval which, although sometimes gratifyingly, even lavishly, bestowed, was all too often withheld. The very word 'approve' crops up noticeably often in the diary, which also bears witness to my frequent, sometimes quite extreme, unhappiness.

A short poem written when I was seventeen reveals an obstinately ambitious, even if determined, streak in my character:

> *If you want a thing so badly*
> *That you'll try with might & main*
> *To get it, & failing the first time,*
> *You'll dare to try again.*
>
> *If you truly crave to have it*
> *So much that you're willing to take*
> *The risk of being laughed at by all men.*
> *And looking a fool for its sake...*

If you go on trying always
And never give in in the fray,
Know this, & so comfort your spirit,
You'll get it for certain one day.

It is clear from a number of entries in my diary that, whatever
I may have felt about my father when I was quite young, by the
time I was a teenager my feelings about him were, to say the
least, mixed. I remember taunting him one Sunday after he
had preached a sermon on reading only edifying literature.
'But Daddy,' I infuriatingly said, 'what about all the Agatha
Christies you keep reading?' (He was a great Agatha fan.) He
was very angry, and my mother rebuked me for being rude to
him. An entry in my diary about my feelings towards my
parents, written in the summer of 1944 when I was fourteen,
runs thus:

I hated Daddy for his attitude [about my having a friend to
stay] — not Mummy because she was sorry for me and I believe
Daddy just twisted her round his finger. Daddy is a little the
intolerant old-fashioned papa with very little real understand-
ing of his children. From things he has said I do not think he
understands Keith & from the fact that he has not — to my
memory — in my hearing said much about Peter implies that
he does not understand him much either. I quite hate Daddy
sometimes as he treats me as *such* a little immature girl whose
ideas do not count. Mummy is not like that, she belongs to a
rather different school of thought, & indeed a different
generation from Daddy.

She was considerably younger than he — and always advised
me not to follow her example and marry young as she had —
which was strange since, as a rule, they were very loyal to each
other vis-à-vis us, their children. We could seldom play off one
against the other.

That I was both quite perceptive about and critical of my
father's proclivities when I was still young (even though as a

little girl I was his pet and played with him quite a lot) is revealed in a diary entry made when I was thirteen:

In bed I was finally overcome by feelings of repulsion towards Daddy because I felt his attitude when beating us had been sadistic and that he liked to think I was wholly 'immature' and incapable of looking after myself, & that his attitude with regard to young girls eg. C., Ann F. and Pam G. (a little) was not quite seemly or kindly towards Mummy.

Despite containing some sympathetic comments on my mother, the diary is littered with accounts of squabbles with her, as well as trouble with my father, and my lamentations over the same. Schoolfriend Ann, it seems, was on one occasion 'shocked as she said I always made my mother out to be horrid', and according to my diary entry for Monday April 17th:

I was listening to a play on the wireless...when Mummy came & hooshed me off to bed. I felt really livid & went slowly to bed with homicidal thoughts wracking my brain. There was a scene. I shook my fist at Mummy, & she yelled from outside the locked bathroom door that she wished she could get at me...I was told I would be in disgrace until I apologised. I decided I would as I had acted foolishly, although Mummy was not wholly blameless either, I would comply with her wishes. However a suitable opportunity never seemed to offer itself, & so presumably I shall always be in disgrace — under the circumstances quite a likely state for me to remain in.

Of the 1944 summer holidays I wrote:

I had a number of rows with Mummy & Daddy concerning bedtime, games after supper etc, which marred the holiday rather. One evening I felt so depressed that I nearly ran away. But as there was nowhere much to run to I forebore, &

instead, wrote a letter full of misery to Keith. The 2 culminating rows occurred just before we came home after only slight aggravation on my part. Mummy wholly lost her temper with me when I did not apologise after bumping into her (It was a clearing up the house day so she had a little excuse.) She gripped my arm like a fanatic & implied that she would not object to the transformation of my living body into a corpse. I felt she acted stupidly & despicably. The next day Daddy pushed me on to the ground because he said the way I walked suggested crossness. [When much younger I used to get into trouble for frowning.] Our angers blazed & Mummy tried to be a son of God by peacemaking between us. Daddy apologised later, but I gave way to my feelings before Peter [with whom I discussed running away — to be a maid — and who, while sympathetic, was not encouraging about this idea].

Biddy's feelings (or lack of same) about me were clearly an endless source of speculation and woe. The following diary entry both contains thoughts about Biddy and reveals views I had about myself at that time:

Sat: March 18th. It was only that night that I fully realised how much I really was within the grip of Biddy's power. Whether she realises what a lot of influence she has over me, I do not know. I do not think she does, as she very rarely tries to exert any authority over me; also from things she has said at different times, indicating that she does not think I care a damn what other people say or think of me, it is evident that she does not think any words of her's would ever turn me from a set purpose. In most ways they (Biddy's words) certainly would affect what I did, but I do not think anything but sound logical argument would turn me from something I felt I ought to do — unless fear of the consequences would. As a matter of a fact people's opinions of me & my actions matter a great deal more to me than people think, but I suppose I do not appear to mind what people say.

That I did mind is clear from various diary entries which report other people's opinions of me and my comments on them. In the course of some party game, Monica A. (who I apparently fancied had a 'pash' on me) knelt to me as the 'prettiest' person present. I quickly added that 'I deplored her bad taste...' Another time I recorded that 'Ann, Biddy & Booker all agreed that my character was intricate and unfathomable — although I personally,' I wrote, 'should not have thought my character was so unduly deep, but it is good if others think so.' And on another occasion I reported that Meg had told me in a letter that 'she felt that one day, somewhere, I was going to be a great success'. Even Miss Popham, the Cheltenham Principal, apparently described me in a letter to my father about my doing an internal scholarship as 'really clever'. However, the letter went on to refer to a 'streak of obstinacy', which evoked the following diary comment: '...personally I should have considered it at least a thick stripe — & amazing of all amazingnesses ended by saying she personally thought I was "quite delightful". (I, & I am sure most others, would consider this an unsuitable way of describing me...)'

My response to the opinion of M., a psychologist family friend, that I was 'a picnoid type' was: 'I suppose M. may be right that I am...as sometimes I seem to get on very smoothly with people & fit in admirably, but under different circumstances I am a very different person & bad at fitting in. I am intraverted, I suppose, as this diary goes to prove.'

Whether or not I was introverted is debatable, but clearly I was apt to get very dejected for one reason or another. On one occasion I wrote that I 'had a chat in the kitchen with Mummy in which I bewailed the fate of women & wished I was a boy. Said that women are just old "bags". They have the dull unpleasant time e.g. looking after the house, having babies etc & they never seem to do the really great deeds & become famous in the same way as men.' Another time I bewailed 'the general seeming impossibility of being righteous & knuckling under to authority.' One afternoon (not long after my expulsion from Stover) 'another fit of extreme depression overtook me...I felt furious about nothing, with nobody, but had a wild feeling I should like to hit or squeeze something hard...I felt rather as if I wanted to bike straight at a brick wall...'

On May 22nd when I was fifteen and in great trouble at school I wrote:

As I lay in bed I felt overcome with the depressing feeling that life is not really worth living. Unless I win fame & cause my name to go down to posterity as a woman who has done great good in the world, I know I shall feel that my life has been a failure. Even if my name does live for ever I probably will not know while I am alive that it is going to. I shall probably never know real peace of mind and tranquility either, as I shall never feel really satisfied with myself and will never feel within me that I should rest as there will be so much left undone that I ought to have done. Life will be either a battle & possible victory, or thwarted ambitions & misery. In either case it will be full of disappointments & never a bed of roses.

21

Although I was always in trouble at school, believed (as we all did) that I longed for the holidays and, when at home, dreaded returning to school, I may well really have been happier there than at home. Despite the petty restrictions of boarding-school life, I was in a sense freer there than at home — or, at any rate, more independent. At school I had to 'stand on my own feet' and 'make my own way'. I looked forward to the holidays as a release from the imprisonment and rules and regulations of school only to find, to my indignation, that my parents imposed almost as many rules as my schoolmistresses. This seemed unjust — surely during the holidays one should be free to do as one liked?

My father promised to take me round the world when I was fourteen, and I lived with this attractive prospect throughout my early childhood — although whether such a trip would ever in fact have taken place is debatable. By the time I was fourteen I had long ceased to be an attractive little girl; my father and I were frequently at loggerheads and I had become decidedly 'bad'. Anyway, by then World War II was in full swing and I heading for university, so it was the Ladies' College instead.

I had, in many ways, really quite enjoyed Stover — much

more than I ever enjoyed Cheltenham. Stover was dreadful, yet fun in a bizarre way; Cheltenham wasn't. I was not even allowed to specialise in my chosen subjects — modern languages, which were what my brothers studied. I was more or less compelled to specialise instead in English and history as I was not deemed good enough at French and German to get to university on the strength of my proficiency in these subjects.

At Cheltenham, as at Farringtons and Stover, I had a bad first couple of terms, then more or less settled down and was happier. Again this must have been partly, as at my two previous schools, because academically I was ahead of my age group so did not seem to fit in anywhere properly for a while. However, as time passed and I stayed on at the school, my age group gradually caught up with me academically. I was in what Cheltenham was too grand to call the VIth Form far too soon and for far too long — from fourteen to eighteen. I should never have been specialising at all as young as fourteen. There were all sorts of basic subjects — science, for instance — that I never studied. My scholastic superiority at all my schools (which was both gratifying and a source of isolation) was not, probably, because I was unduly intelligent; rather it was because of my early start with Nanny, which meant I was apt to be ahead of my age group and youngest in the class — as well as in the family.

One or two poems written at the time, as well as diary items, illustrate how I felt about Cheltenham — for instance one written in 1944, which suprisingly perhaps, considering how uncomplimentary it was about the school, got printed in St. Austin's magazine:

A New Girl's Impressions of Coll'

The first few days by new girls spent
At almost any schools
Are not too good as all the time
They feel such utter fools.

The new at Coll, worse luck,
Are in this same unhappy state.
To wander lost & vaguely stare
Is their unhappy fate.

Until one seventeen summers is
One's hair one must not curl,
But cut it off or crop it short
Just like a little girl.

One's body nude must ne'er be seen
For that is not quite done
At Cheltenham Coll, where one must be
As modest as a nun.

And if one late for meals is
Oneself one must excuse.
About the house one ne'er must run
In muddy outdoor shoes.

Virginia Frith, St. Austin's head,
Must treated be politely
For Vige's word, so I've heard tell,
'Must not be taken lightly.'

The other girls who are not new
They have both friends and fun,
And so I'll not be sorry
When my new-girl days are done.

A mock-heroic poem I wrote when I was sixteen also says something about the school and my opinion of it:

A Day at College

And now that night is driven from the skies
And Phoebus 'gins in golden light to rise
The silence cleaved is by that doleful knell
Which College maidens call the Rising Bell.
Immediately the skies are rent with noise,
More loud than even mighty Achilles' voice,
As he, exulting with triumphant joy,
Dragged vanquished Hector round the walls of Troy.
They shout of Philip's wars & battles won,
Of $x + h$ & Latin preps undone.
But some frail mortals, overcome with sleep,
Recumbant still remain in slumbers deep,
Until, disguised in robes of purest white,
In cap & apron – O unwelcome sight!
Arising from the infernal depths below
Appears mankind's most fearful deadly foe,
Who, with rough hands, casts back the bedclothes warm,
And leaves uncovered every shivering form.
'Ye beauteous maidens lying neath the spell
Laid on you by the rulers of deep Hell,
Know this, that you must stay beneath their sway
And scrupulously College rules obey.
So now I bid you do what I command
And never more deserve my reprimand.
Rise up at once e'er it becomes too late.
Behold the time piece says it's nearly eight.
If in five minutes you may not be seen
Neatly arrayed in College vesture green
The penalty that you will surely pay
Will be to eat your bread ungreased all day.'
She says, & goes out with a thundering crash.

Immediately the waters 'gin to splash.
The air is filled with clouds of soapy foam
Like salt seas driven in a mighty storm.
Ablutions done, the maidens fair array
Their graceful forms in honour of the fray
In which, perforce, they will too soon engage
With tiresome foes, right powerful & brave,
The which are known as anti-logarithms,
Subjunctive moods & endless Papal Schisms.
Their bodies they adorn in dazzling green,
Which glimmers with a sparkling tweedlike sheen.
Their necks they gird with stripy silken scarves,
And lisle fabrics cover their slim calves.
With divers silks their flowing locks they bind
Into tight bunches hanging down behind.
But ah, alas, it is their doleful fate
That they shall not be ready till too late.
At last the cursèd silvery notes resound
Which, by their noise, the half-dressed girls confound,
Who, in distress, cry out:– 'O spiteful Hell!
For surely we have heard the Silence Bell'.
Their doleful cry reaches the shades below
And Matron's face a crimson hue does glow,
More red than e'en that fatal ruddy star
Which, with its light, foretells disease & war.
She rises up with clamour in her train
And enters in the dormitory again.
Her fatal doom with stern resolve is uttered.
That day the girls must eat their bread unbuttered.

(At about this time as well as doing Latin I was reading Alexander Pope in English.)

Diary items written during my early days at Cheltenham are comments on the school as well as descriptions and explanations of my initial unhappiness there, and they bear out the points made in the poems. My account of my first term includes the following remarks:

My first term at Cheltenham was, like all terms, in parts pleasant & in parts unpleasant. Although I was by no means wretched all the time, yet on the whole I have so far taken a dim view of C.L.C. There are far too many rules & regulations, & one can scarcely move without self-interrogation on the legitimacy of one's action. On being 'taken out' one cannot go to shows of any description, in public conveyances, in the High St., in the road by the Boys' Coll' or in any of the exciting sort of cafés where one is able to listen to squeaking fiddles & eat poached eggs on toast. Everyone is very good & exceedingly modest. Good deportment is considered such a vital quality to possess that one scarcely feels — or should scarcely feel — the back of a chair from one end of the term to the other. It is now approximately 3 weeks before the end of the spring term and I have now arrived at the great age of 15.

Although so long after my coming to Coll' I still seem to have written scarecely anything about life in general here. As was almost inevitable — for me anyhow — my 1st term was rather lonely. I don't think I was disliked but people just did not do those things which are essential to make someone, who feels 'new' a pretty long time, feel at home — bagging places for one at meals or walking to Coll' with one etc. Matters were not remedied by the fact that I am in U.C.2c — a class containing nobody from S.A but myself, and I was in a dormitory consisting of S.C year people barring the pre's [prefects] & the head of one of the sides...

This term I am in a dorm with my own year & people are all much friendlier.

However an entry made at the beginning of the following term is full of gloom:

May 3rd–8th. [1945] Black dejection. Although my 3rd term everything seemed far worse than ever before. On the 4th

Heather & I went for quite a long walk into the country but even she soon ceased from being in the least friendly. I did not really care as I do not think she is a startlingly interesting or exciting person, but still she was just somebody. I just had a feeling of being completely unwanted by anybody. Nobody bagged me places at meals or ever evinced an even remote desire for my company...

I felt lonely & so acted rather foolishly & childishly...I remember feeling almost more miserable dejected & unwanted than ever before, wrote a letter home which was one long drawn out tale of woe about Coll' & more especially S.A, how I did not think it fair that I should spend the greater part of the rest of my schooldays in a place I hated, & in which I begged Mummy & Daddy to do something about it, let me leave, come down & see me, or 'something'...

I was very nearly expelled from Cheltenham as well as Stover — for running away and going down town on Victory Night. My father came and pleaded with Miss Popham, so in the end I was only 'suspended'. My scholarship was taken away and I was expelled from St. Austin's. For half a term I was segregated as a moral invalid in the school sanatorium, initially being kept more or less incommunicado as far as fellow pupils were concerned. It was my first taste of imprisonment. I was gradually allowed back into circulation (although with all school treats forbidden for the rest of term), and by the end of my time at Cheltenham had been housed in six different places. The diary includes a detailed account of my Victory Day — and night — escapades and ensuing incarceration:

VE Day. May 8th. This day will certainly always be a day which I shall think of as heavily underlined & in black letters. At the beginning of the term 'Popeye' had given out that in honour of VE Day which was bound to soon occur we were to have 3 days extra summer holiday instead of 3 days during the term & that on the day itself there would be 2 hours work, & an afternoon & evening, (not in the town of course but at houses or Field) conducted with 'quietness and restraint'. I considered the idea of 3 days extra in the summer to be all very well, but by that time VE Day celebrations would all be over, & inwardly & in fact outwardly too... I implied that by hook or by crook I intended seeing the fun on VE Day even if it entailed running away in the afternoon. I am sure they did not take what I said seriously, nor yet the 'High Command' to whom I implied much the same in my doleful letter.

I will now record the day's events (they actually continued into the small hours of the following day.) I went to College as usual in the morning. Prayers were drawn out into a short VE Day thanks-giving service & several people felt faint in consequence. [We were forbidden to wear red, white and blue rosettes to prayers, presumably because this would have been unladylike.] After prayers we were supposed to work for 2 hours, either at our houses or at College. I went back to the house, unlike most, & did no work, possibly unlike most, but instead wrote a VE Day poem.

V.E. Day

Is it over, truly over?
Is the battle really won?
Are the days of hardship over
And the nights of terror done?
But the answer comes back: 'Never
Till the final set of sun'.

But the ac-ac guns are silent
And the smoke has cleared away.
The moaning planes drone homewards
And the skies no more are grey
But a voice says: 'Cease not fighting
While evil still holds sway.'

But the tortured starved & captive
Are being succoured & released.
The shrieks & crashing rockets
And the blazing fires have ceased.
But a voice says: 'Keep your patience
Till there's victory in the East.'

There is no cause for rejoicing
While the dying lie in pain,
When cities have been ruined,
And there's weeping for the slain,
While sin is still unconquered,
And wars will come again.

For until our human nature
Obtains wisdom from the skies
Another Adolph Hitler
In a different disguise
Is certain in the future
To once again arise.

So if you make your bonfires
I bid you still to pray
For the wounded, sad & homeless,
But especially for the day
When wisdom right & justice
Throughout the world hold sway.

Rain poured down. As nobody would be doing anything in the afternoon & Field in the evening was optional I had decided that unless some unforeseen incident arose I should not be missed by a soul in the house if I went out after lunch & did not return until supper time. I was quite right, I spent a most enjoyable afternoon (the weather turned sunny) breaking practically every College rule in existance without a soul — except for Stubbs to whom I imparted my misdeeds — being the wiser. I obtained permission from Gar' to collect my byke from station & as I really was not sure as to whether it were a crime to go for it alone, I decided that I could [not] feel quite safe until I had got it. I went in my blue mufti raincoat — quite permissable as Mummy had not sent my tweed coat — & took my old Stover panama, which might later, so I thought, come in useful as a disguise. Eventually I felt so uncomfortable & unbecoming in it that I did not wear it much.

After I had left the house I had that deliciously free happy & adventurous feeling which I always have when I am breaking rules & there is a bit of a risk, & the feeling was enhanced by the delightful knowledge that I had a whole afternoon before me & that I had burst College fetters assunder, defied authority, was being supremely unladylike, (I ran some of the way to the station) & was doing something which probably nobody else in College would even dream of doing. To my great dejection my byke did not seem to have materialised at Lansdown Station, & so I treked off to Malvern Rd which is the sort of station to which the only means of access is over the railway lines by whose sides sundry notices stand declaring the illegitimacy of crossing the lines. I crossed them.

I was not really surprised to find my bicycle was not there, & as time was running on, I caught a convenient bus to St James'. The conducteress appeared to be taking a holiday, at any rate she collected no fare from me, — to my relief as I only had a halfpenny and a 10/- note. For some completely obscure reason I did discover my byke at St. James' (reason obscure as St James' is the G.W.R. station & my byke had come on the L.M.S. line from Bristol — at least I thought it had.) A friendly porter pumped it up for me & I fixed my patriotic emblem on the front.

The best patriotic emblem I had been able to muster was the red 'Fiend' [a fiendish cloth doll my mother had had as a child] with white wool & a blue hair ribbon twined around him. He was apparently considered an original emblem as people stared at & remarked on him — rather to my discomfit as I could not be sure that a Coll' staff unknown to me, but self not unknown to her, might not be staring.

I bicycled into the town not feeling quite sure what to do & nearly bumping into swarming people. The town was crowded with laughing summer-clad people and flags, some of which were waving from windows & some suspended over streets. Every girl seemed to have red white & blue ribbon in her hair & a male attendant — frequently the latter was of U.S. origine. I felt hot & silly in my mac, & hat & took them off so that I rode about in a mufti blouse & skirt. In the end I decided to byke out to Southam, but on the way I passed the 'Gaumont' cinema where the much advertised 'Wilson' was on. I went to see it. The film was no doubt wonderful from a historical point of view, but to my mind & mood seemed a bit too historical & therefore slightly heavy going. Throughout the show I had a slightly gnawing feeling of apprehension that possibly my absence had been noticed at the house.

I was in luck that afternoon as I arrived about 20 minutes before the show began, got quite a decent seat at a reasonable price & did not arrive during the middle of the film. There was VE Day news which consisted mainly in salutes to all the forces accompanied by much clapping & cheering in which I joined quite exuberantly. We heard Churchill's broadcast speech at 3. The show was over by about 5.30. & I then cycled off to Southam to wish the Aunts a happy VE Day.

It did not seem as though it had been a particularly happy VE Day for them. Aunty Rosy seemed very harassed & for some veiled reason (veiled to me in spite of involved explanations from her) felt she could not have Peter over the weekend but was wiring to tell him to go to Geoffrey's in Cheltenham. Aunty Rosy rambled on talking for hours not letting me get a word in edgewise but at last she took me over to see Aunt Angela, Christine & child (Anna & her child were away.) As the household had been ravaged by measles Aunt Angela seemed all tired and overworked but managed to muster together some eatables and drinkable for me. Christine, (looking haggard, quite unrecognisable, & rather like Manty) & child, (curly haired, one year old, not nearly as nice as Paul & coldly disdainful of me) were infectious but rashless after measles.

Having been a measles victim in days gone by, also the preceeding term an epidemic had given the disease to probably anyone who would get it (anyway in the house) I decided it would not much matter if I did see Christine. I stayed & talked until 6.30 recounting my afternoon's misdeeds, which did not appear to shock them greatly, then I byked back.

I cycled up & then down the High Street [which was out of bounds] & listened to a brass band on the Prom for a minute or 2 & then returned to the house shortly before supper. After supper I listened to the King's broadcast & did nothing much until bedtime. As I was getting ready for bed I suddenly realised that the evening was the time when most of the VE Day fun would take place, & quite suddenly I decided to break loose & go down town after lights. Now this may seem stark madness, & true I was feeling in an adventurous headstrong mood, but the chances of my getting caught were exceedingly remote as not a soul would dream of anyone quitting the house after lights even on VE Night. All I had to do was to partially dress, put on my dressing gown, slip quietly downstairs go out through a playroom or drawing room window, & make off, under cover of bushes as far as possible.

Being VE Night there was a racket in the dorm which seemed liable to last, & people were talking about such tantalisations as bonfires, fireworks & cheering on the Prom. Suddenly I decided to ask Stubbs to come with me. She politely declined my offer & apparently did not think for one moment that I was being serious (Cannot imagine why as she knows quite well how capable I am of rule breaking, moreover I was asking for her company in complete seriousness. In every way for her & myself it was a good job she did not come.)[1] As time was getting on & the dorm failing to settle

[1] In fact, as I later learned, it was she who, albeit initially incredulous about my scheme, eventually told the authorities about it when my absence had been noted. It seems she was desperately worried lest disaster might have befallen me if I had really gone on a nocturnal spree down town.

down I decided to go after leaving Stubbs — sometime between 10 and 10.30 I believe.

All went according to plan. Partially dressed & with my dressing gown on I sneaked & squeaked downstairs, got through a playroom window I had left open for the purpose, & slipped into the bushes, where I put on my grey skirt and short brown coat & slung my bag over my shoulder. I did not cope with the bush problems & my exit from the garden frightfully efficiently & was a little afraid I had been seen by people looking out of windows. Apparently these fears were unfounded. I went out through the gate near the bicycle sheds, put on my shoes & walked off into the town, where, although I missed the fireworks & the bonfires, (latter on the outskirts of town,) I had an amazing time.

I wandered on the Prom. in a desultory manner for a bit. Buildings were flood light, street lamps shone out, flags added splashes of blue, green & scarlet & above everything was the starry sky, dead black as seen from the light-up street. Crowds swarmed everywhere in pairs, families or gangs. People sang and danced in the streets. Actually I felt a little lonely & half wished to pick up a jolly Yank — not from a sexual point of view, but because I should have liked company & the novel & criminal (in the eyes of the well brought up) experience. Actually I paid little attention to the remarks made at me by any males, as I felt in a way rather shy & out of my element in that throng.

Wandering in the Prom. & vaguely wondering what to do, I came upon a jeep which was carrying a cargo of humans of every size & sex. The jeep stopped, the cargo removed itself, & another, including myself, installed itself. The jeep was so covered that the driver could not see in front of him & was ages starting. It was the maddest ride I have been for. I was precariously perched at the back & vaguely wondered whether I was going to fall off or whether the jeep would crash into something. It did veer right off the road on to some grass at one juncture. We drove further & further away from the centre of the town with frequent halts & removals of cargoe.

In the end we seemed miles from the Prom. & High Street, & when only five girls & three Yanks remained who sang songs I did not know, & when the driver spent more time kissing than driving, I decided to cease trying to delude myself into thinking I was highly enjoying myself, as by that time I had ceased to, & instead unloaded myself & made my way back to the High Street. As I was making my way down it a dishevelled youth, who I have a vague idea may have been cross-eyed, disentangled himself from his comrades & asked me if he could take me home. As I was not sure what else to do I agreed, but did not go back to the house straight away.

We wandered about the streets watching the dense dancing & singing crowds. I was glad that he did not seem all lovey dovey & that his voice was — unlike most Yanks I have talked to — intelligible. We talked about one thing & another in quite an ordinary way, & I rather unwisely told him about my breaking out of school etc. I did not gather very much about him, but apparently he was 17, & an engineer — I do not even know his name. He was quite obviously — luckily — as inexperienced in the art of love making as myself, & it was only when we were about to turn back, & were in a park where Yanks & girls lay sprawling revoltingly on the grass locked in each other's arms, that he very tentatively asked if he could put his arm round me. Knowing how hopeless arguement would prove, & anyway rather wanting the novel experience of marching round a town at about midnight with a completely unknown youth's arm round me, I let him do so. Just outside the gate by the bicycle shed through which I had made my exit from the garden he asked if I would kiss him good night. I gave him a brief kiss & was just departing when he demanded a proper one. I argued a bit but there seemed nothing for it, & so in the end I found myself standing with his lips pressed firmly against mine for a second or 2. I cannot say the action awakened any hidden wells of emotion or one spark of sexual excitement, still it was an experience & one which probably most girls of my age & standing have not had, and therefore it was a good thing.

After the boy had gone I was just about to enter by the gate I had come out of when I thought I heard someone coming & so moved back round the corner, & finally went in by the other gate. I spent ages searching for my dressing gown among the bushes & practically decided to come out first thing the next day and get it. I found it at last, & had just got back through the playroom when 3 things happened simultaneously. (a.) The drawing room door opened (b.) A torch with seemingly nothing behind it appeared. (c.) I experienced internal unpleasant feelings & in the same second decided to try & hide & decided to stay put. Gar's voice [the voice of Miss Garside, St. Austin's 'house-lady' — we had nothing so plebeian as 'house-mistresses' at Cheltenham] demanded, to my mind quite superfluously, what I was doing. I replied, quite superfluously, that I was just coming in. Gar' immediately phoned 'Popeye' & then pessimistically remarking that I had ruined my career marched me off to a dorm, in Middle House, where there was a vacant bed. Jean Elliott woke up, & when Gar' — I cannot think why — had gone I gave her an account of most of my doings. (I have not told anyone about my male chaperon.)

Oddly enough, although it was ages before I fell asleep, I felt quite philosophical about the whole business. For a few seconds when Gar' had just nabbed me I had had a more dead than alive feeling, but as I lay in bed I did not feel very apprehensive, unhappy or remorseful. I had been intensely miserable that term & had felt that even expulsion would be a happy release from Coll'. I had prayed to Mummy & Daddy to do something about it, & now something had happened. If I were expelled or suspended it would mean going home to Peter, strawberries & the sea; & even if I were sacked I might be able to go to some other school, or if not, later I could get into Exeter University on matric & take a London degree there. At any rate something had, I felt, happened. Nothing could have been much worse than it had been, & my name would at least gain a little notice and notoriety in the house. I should be discussed & talked about, & even if not favourably,

I would really rather unpleasant things were said than nothing at all. Over & above all this was, I suppose, that owing to all the scrapes I have got into & the moments of excruciating apprehension that I have experienced, I have become hardened & feel blasé about even the worst school punishments. There is something very satisfactory about such a state — at any rate it reduces agony of mind.

VE Day the 2nd: May 9th – May 20th. Pretty much what I had expected happened. I was whisked off to see Pop' after breakfast with Gar' who tried to probe me for details of what I had done. I have written so many letters & seem to have talked so much about all my VE Day doings, the results of the same & my & other people's opinions of myself, my activities & Cheltenham Ladies College as related to me, that now I feel so sick of the whole subject that I shall not write much about it. I was not expelled but have been suspended for the term which I am spending here at the San. Daddy came whisking up post haste & thinks that the fact that I have not been expelled is entirely due to him — Mummy believes so anyhow, — but I think Pop' had practically decided only to suspend me after she had seen me before Daddy came. Gar lectured me & added deceit onto the list of my crimes. Davey — the San matron [Miss Davison, who was also Miss Popham's close friend — perhaps the reason for the occasional placing of miscreants in her hands for reformation] — has catechised me & wangled out a brief autobiography for Popey's benefit.

I have had 2 sessions with the all powerful principal. The first on VE Day 2nd only a brief interview during which she managed, however, to find out about my visit to Southam [which was a cause of considerable concern because of the measles]. During the 2nd interview, a week or so later, I told her the misdeeds that I had not mentioned before, under instigation although not exactly pressure, from the High Command. I have managed to keep my male companion practically out of the picture. Throughout I stuck to the truth except for one lie to Gar' where truth might, I felt, have got

Stubbs into the soup. On the whole it has not been all as awful as it might. I think that quite probably I shall dislike this term no more than one at St Austin's, & I am not returning there next term. I think I should do far better at some more free & easy school — anyhow strict discipline seems to have failed. Unfortunately Pop' has taken my life into her own hands and refuses to recommend me anywhere but another such school as this.

My 2nd interview with Pop was not too bad in parts. She drew quite a bright picture of a diplomatic or journalistic career for me, & ended by shaking hands & saying she believed in me. Davey, with whom I had long arguments, said one or 2 cheering things as well. Although I felt sorry & miserable when I saw Daddy, who seemed terribly cut up, yet I do not really feel repentant, & am trying to follow Kiplings advice & 'having made one heap of all my winnings (scholarship & grant included) & risked them on one turn of pitch & toss & lost' I am trying 'to start again at my beginnings never breathing a word about my loss' (the latter unfortunately difficult as others do more than breathe about it.) It may be selfish but it is true to say that I do not regret what I did, as I should never have forgiven myself if I had not celebrated in some way on VE Day. I would take the risk again — it was only a very slight risk as had the unforeseen not arisen I should never have been caught (the unforeseen as I later discovered was the fact that Packy happened to glance into my cu' [dormitory cubicle] which she found empty.) What I am chiefly sorry for is (a.) the wretchedness I have caused at home (b.) the loss of my scholarship & grant which Gran is making up to Daddy out of what is — if any is left — going to be a legacy to me. (c.) I am not, for some obscure reason, going to be allowed to go to Oxford next hols. I was not going to have been allowed to come under the evil influence of Biddy in the summer either, but on receiving a letter pleading the good influence Biddy exerted on my behalf plus letters from her (the sending of which went terribly against the grain) to prove what I said, Daddy wrote to say he would 'reconsider his decision.'

I have had a lot of mail. Letters from Mummy, Daddy & Peter written before VE Day, & later letters sermonising me. Peter's later letter was not a sermon & he did not mention my evil deeds, but merely sorrow at the impossibility of our meeting at the weekend (a great blow) & containing £1 to make up, — good old Peter. [He did however write me quite a disquietingly stern letter later — unlike Keith who wrote to say he had been ordered to send me another sermon but was disinclined to do so. According to a later diary entry 'all he blaimed me for in my VE Day celebrations was letting myself get caught (I entirely agree)'. According to Peter though 'my misdeeds had caused great distress at home. Daddy had aged, & he, Peter, had been obliged to support Mummy when she was told of my follies'.]

I have also received a parcel from home & sundry ones from the house, also quite a nice note from Gar' saying that in many ways I had made quite a good beginning in the house. I myself wrote a lot of letters, & I heard from Prune & Jean Duncan, also Stubbs, whose verdict was that I had been a 'suicidal B.F.' & Roseabelle who apparently thought me a plucky dare devil idiot, but who seemed to think, goodness knows why, that good was likely to come out of all this business. [I had been enjoined not to talk about what I had done to any of my fellow pupils.] Finally I have had a letter from the Archbishop of Canterbury to whom I had sent a copy of my VE Day poem because a desire had suddenly come over me to do something with it, & I vaguely hoped it might somehow find its way into print. It neither has nor will to my knowledge, but I received quite an appreciative letter from the Archbishop.

It is not too bad here though as time has run on I have grown less & less enthusiastic about life here & often when seated alone in my room feel a cross between an invalid & a suet pudding. I have met one or 2 quite pleasant convalescers with whom I have got on well & I have sat & eaten in the garden on sunny days. Lately there have not been any convalescers & I have spent much time alone in my room doing Latin (I go to Coll' for Latin coaching) [2] or reading the copious history books with which Owen snows me under. Food is good but I get hungry owing to large gaps between the meals. The garden is bursting with fruit, strawberries — round which I yesterday did some strawing — included. I can bath every night have breakfast in bed & work pretty much at my own speed — things might be worse.

I began one painting which, unfinished, I demolished. I have been told I shall be able to sketch & go for byke rides with Nurse sometimes but I do not seem, as yet anyway, to be allowed to tramp off alone for long walks. Unfortunately I am already getting very used to the fine extensive view from the top of Leckhampton Hill [the school sanatorium was at the foot of this Cotswold hill], & as I shall probably see it practically every day from now until the end of term there is no knowing what my final attitude towards it will be. Davey seemed pleasant enough to begin with but now I seem to be veering from her good books as I isolate myself too much in my bedroom for her liking [she once said ruefully I would never have any friends]. I think she is rather an illogical woman. She is nauseatingly anxious for me to 'make friends' at College & yet hates me to have any dealings with Margaret rather a nice maid — or next best (worst I mean) thing to a maid — here. One day she was annoyed that I had spent all the afternoon in my room doing history, & another day because I had spent 2 hours rambling innocently up on 'Lecky' (having been told to go for a walk). It is quite beastly the way she, Pop', parents & everyone want 'to do their best' for me. This 'doing of best' operation strikes me as likely to be 'all for the worst' for myself & everyone else in the long run. Already Davey has got on to the track of my lack of graciousness & sociability (— if not here — I think on the whole I am quite a sociable being), & anyway there is nothing much to talk to Davey & the staff

---

[2] I was trying to cram four years' Latin into four terms in order to add it to my School Certificate, this being necessary if I were to go to university.

here about, besides which I have plenty of work & so on to keep me fully occupied, not leaving much time for rushing round saying superfluous hullos to people (as Davey suggests) especially as when having said hello there would be nothing further to say.) Anyhow I must try & keep on the right side of Davey & the other staff.

There is a lot more I could write but I shall not... A great craving to get a motor byke for when I am 16 assailed me & I have written to Keith asking him to loan me some cash.[3] I will make one more remark than I said I would. According to the head of the D.S. house — an attractive, seemingly rather jolly girl who came here today (May 20th) with another D.S. girl — Davey is sorry for me & thinks I am a 'lonely girl.' I also gathered from this girl that St. Austin's is notorious for ignoring new girls & generally not helping them to settle down.

* * *

Some weeks later I was allowed to return to College for classes every day — after first being visited at the Sanatorium by the Senior Prefect, who delivered a homily and was plainly much more embarrassed by the situation than I. Then at about half-term I was sent to a new house. Thereafter life at Cheltenham, although still far from perfect, improved greatly.

[3] In fact, throughout my adult life, the only motor vehicles I have ever possessed have been some form of motor cycle.

22

My Cheltenham career ended strangely. Eventually, after pleading in a rather degrading way with Miss Popham, I was made a House Prefect over the head of my current House-lady. It was an odd role for me to have — trying to get my fellow pupils to keep the rules. I was probably not very good at the job: I kept telling others not to run up and down stairs then did so myself when no one was looking. However I achieved the small privileges and slight prestige that went with being a House Prefect (there was never any question of my being anything so august as a College Prefect).

Then I did university scholarship exams. I acquitted myself badly, failing at first to get even a place anywhere, much less a scholarship.

One day I learned to my surprise that I had won a scholarship to Exeter University. There seemed no point in staying on at school, and my father, never one to waste money, agreed. So I went to Miss Popham and said: 'I think I'll leave on Tuesday.' Somewhat taken aback, she replied: 'Oh, do stay.' Perhaps she really meant it. 'No, I don't think I will,' I replied, and I didn't. She kissed me goodbye and I went home that Tuesday and became a waiter in Paignton. A month or two later I went to Cambridge (not Exeter after all) and read history. I was eighteen. My childhood was over.

also by Pat Arrowsmith:

JERICHO

Written and first published in the early 1960s, this is a novel of the early 'peace camps' — the direct action against the Bomb that Pat Arrowsmith helped to create. A tale of conflict between women and men, heterosexual and gay, pacifists and socialists, this 'tough-minded and impressive book' (*Observer*) well conveys the ambiguous atmosphere of a time of change.
0 946097 08 9   UK £3.95 US $7.50

SOMEWHERE LIKE THIS

Pat Arrowsmith's second novel is set in Holloway Prison, where the author was frequently interned, and where she also wrote *Jericho*. As a love story between a butch young burglar and a fluffy first offender, it was controversial when first issued in 1970 (though the *Sun* called it 'riveting'), but became a minor classic of dyke history when reprinted twenty years later.
0 85449 143 0   UK £5.95 US $10.95

another new title from Heretic Books:

Kath Clements
WHY VEGAN

World food crisis! Doubling of Earth's population by the year 2025! Still not made the connection — well open the pages of this classic book and enlighten yourself. In this completely updated edition, Kath Clements explains why veganism is so central to a sustainable lifestyle. Veganism boosts your body and sense of well-being through a health-giving diet of purely vegetable origin. And by ending your cruel exploitation of animals for food and other products, veganism uplifts your spirit, and directly connects you to the struggle for survival on our stricken planet.
0 946097 30 5   UK £6.95 US $10.95